S0-BDP-504

ALCTS Papers on Library Technical Services & Collections, #13

Managing Electronic Resources: Contemporary Problems and Emerging Issues

EDITORS

Pamela Bluh and *Cindy Hepfer*

Association for Library Collections & Technical Services
American Library Association
Chicago   2006

Z
692
C65M36
2006

c.1

63274885   9-10-0

Association for Library Collections & Technical Services (ALCTS)
ALCTS is a division of the American Library Association

ALCTS Publishing
50 E. Huron St.
Chicago, IL 60611
www.ala.org/alcts

Library of Congress Cataloging-in-Publication Data
　　Managing electronic resources : contemporary problems and emerging
issues / Pamela Bluh and Cindy Hepfer, editors.
　　　　p.　cm. — (ALCTS papers on library technical services and collections ; #13)
　　Includes bibliographical references.
　　ISBN 0-8389-8366-9
　　1. Libraries–Special collections–Electronic information resources. 2. Electronic
information resources–Management. I. Bluh, Pamela M.　II. Hepfer, Cindy.
III. Series: ALCTS papers on library technical services and collections ; no. 13.
　　Z692.C65M36 2006
　　025.17'4–dc22

Copyright © 2006 by the American Library Association. All rights reserved except those
which may be granted by Sections 107 and 108 of the Copyright Revision Act of 1976.

09　08　07　06　　4　3　2　1

Contents

Introduction

PAMELA BLUH and
CINDY HEPFER

In the last few years there has been an explosion of interest in electronic resources, centering largely on the aspects of ordering; crafting agreements with publishers, aggregators, and vendors; and establishing gateways and portals to access the new material. The resources in their many guises—indexing and abstracting databases often include full-text articles, e-journals, e-books, and digitized and born-digital documents—have become virtually ubiquitous in library collections. As the details surrounding electronic resources mount, librarians urgently need to identify and introduce practical solutions for managing these collections.

The Association for Library Collections & Technical Services (ALCTS) recognized this dilemma and, at the 2003 Midwinter Meeting of the American Library Association (ALA), presented a symposium titled "Managing Electronic Resources: Meeting the Challenge," which served as a forum where the issues surrounding electronic resources were addressed. Capitalizing on the interest generated by that first session, a second symposium "Taming the Electronic Tiger: Effective Management of E-resources" was held in San Diego at the ALA 2004 Midwinter Meeting. Because the second symposium created even more enthusiasm for the subject, it seems altogether fitting that the presentations from these two meetings should be gathered together to form the nucleus of a publication on the subject of electronic resources management (ERM). Several invited papers augment the discussion and offer readers additional insights into the complexities of managing collections of electronic resources.

As electronic resources mature and evolve, the need for effective management becomes evermore critical. Librarians must reconcile the desire for access to an expanding number of resources with the realities of managing the collection in a fiscally responsible manner. To come to grips with these seemingly diametrically opposite demands, librarians require a single mechanism that will enable them to gather, analyze, and interpret data about these resources so that a comprehensive picture of the collection can be obtained. The Midwinter symposia were designed to describe the existing and emerging management options and provide librarians with practical suggestions for dealing with this multifaceted subject. This publication offers both an overview of the current e-resources landscape and detailed discussions of specific aspects of electronic resources.

Sandy Hurd's paper "The Challenges of Electronic Resources Management, or a Primer in Tiger Taming" uses a broad-brush approach in considering the changes that will be necessary to manage electronic resources successfully. Timothy D. Jewell asks "Electronic Resource Management Systems: What Should They Do?" and answers the question by describing some of the events and activities that shaped the development of the Digital Library Federation's Electronic Resource Management Initiative.

Beth Forrest Warner's piece "Managing Electronic Resources in Today's Integrated Library Management System Environment" posits the idea that the functionality of the integrated library system, combined with third-party functionality, could be one solution for obtaining a comprehensive package of ERM services. By contrast, Dan Tonkery explores the role of the subscription agent as the manager of electronic resources. His paper "The Three A's of E-resource Management: Aggravation, Agitation, and Aggregation" describes some of the headaches librarians face when dealing with e-resources. Tonkery believes that subscription agents possess the technical expertise, the necessary business acumen, and the financial resources to develop and market a viable alternative for managing electronic resources.

Norm Medeiros's paper "House of Horrors: Exorcising Electronic Resources" considers the universe of e-resource management systems and describes the experience of one consortium in developing a tailor-made management system. But management of electronic resources encompasses more than bibliographic and fiscal control and an interpretation of statistics. In his paper "Why Aren't Librarians More KISSable? Keeping Electronic Resources Management User-Centered," Tim Bucknall moves the discussion from a technical perspective to an examination of the access and service issues with which librarians must deal. He suggests that some of the procedures that have been introduced in the name of efficiency are, upon close inspection, counterproductive in terms of accessibility.

For ERM to be successful on a variety of levels, it must be standards-based. Friedemann Weigel writes eloquently and convincingly in "Taming the Tiger Technologically: Through the Standards Jungle (and out Again Unscathed!)" about the importance—and the attendant difficulties—of establishing a solid standards platform for ERM. Robert Molyneux, in "Making Sense of User

Statistics: First the Bad News," examines the rapidly changing standards landscape and the complications this presents for obtaining valid, useful statistical data. Jennifer Weintraub's contribution, "Usage Statistics at Yale University Library: A Case Study," discusses the value of obtaining and maintaining statistics for collection assessment and development and budgeting, as well as the difficulties that this challenge poses.

In the excitement of acquiring electronic resources it is easy to forget other aspects of ERM. George Machovec's paper "Preservation of Digital Resources" and Paula D. Watson's "Who Will Keep Print in the Digital Age? Current Thinking on Shared Repositories" should serve as reminders of another dimension of ERM. As librarians reduce their print collections and more and more heavily rely on digital collections, they should be mindful of the consequences of this approach for the future.

Rounding out the publication is Richard W. Boss's synopsis of the requirements for an electronic management system.

The subject of ERM is diverse and dynamic and this publication attempts to expose that diversity and dynamism while simultaneously offering a number of concrete suggestions for controlling those resources. As new developments in ERM develop and multiply, this book also will serve as a snapshot of how librarians and others in the information industry were coping with and thinking about ERM.

The Challenges of Electronic Resources Management, or a Primer in Tiger Taming

SANDY HURD

Here is the tiger. He has long, sharp claws and very sharp teeth. He is fearsome. He is lithe and, like all cats, moves very quickly and easily. He cannot be tamed or managed like an ordinary tabby cat. Electronic resources, like the tiger, can strike fear into the heart of even the bravest librarian. And like the tiger, electronic resources cannot be managed like familiar, traditional print resources in the library's collection. Librarians must find new ways to manage and tame those resources, and to do that librarians must change the way they manage their collections. They can no longer stay behind the scenes and continue to work in the same old ways. If electronic resources are going to be managed and integrated successfully into collections, new methods must be found to handle the work.

In thinking about electronic resources management (ERM) today, one should look beyond a single e-journal or a single module and broadly consider ERM. As part of that examination, one must keep in mind not only the capabilities of today's integrated library systems (ILS) but also the in-house management capabilities developed by many libraries, such as Access files, Excel spreadsheets, and locally created databases. The way that electronic resources are used and how they are presented to users—through library and institutional Web pages—must be kept in mind at all times. In short, both technical and public service factors must be considered when a library decides how to manage its electronic resources.

No single definition for electronic resources has yet been proposed or adopted. An electronic resource can be a single journal, a package of journals,

This paper is based on a presentation made at the ALCTS Midwinter Symposium "Taming the Electronic Tiger: Effective Management of Electronic Resources," held in San Diego, January 2004.

a full-text database, an abstracting and indexing file, an image database, or a licensed set of CD-ROMs. Despite these variations, electronic resources share two common characteristics:

- acquiring them requires new procedures, and
- accessing them requires new mechanisms.

Part of managing electronic resources efficiently has to do with changing the image and role of the librarian. This may be quite uncomfortable for librarians because it means giving up safe, predictable procedures and behaviors. It is no longer acceptable to be simply a reference librarian or a serials cataloger. In today's fast-paced information community, everyone has to learn to be an effective manager, whether it be of people or resources. Librarians need to understand the budgetary implications of acquiring electronic resources and the importance of managing collections in a businesslike manner. Acquiring electronic resources is now complex and costly, which means that librarians need a new set of skills to simultaneously operate in the public arena and behind the scenes. In both instances, keeping the end user in mind is imperative.

The principal venue for presentation of resources is a library's Web site. If one examines the Web sites of a dozen libraries—public, private, academic, and special—one will recognize some excellent designs that are easy to understand, navigate, and use. Obviously good work has been done behind the scenes. There are some bad designs as well, where navigation is difficult and definitely not intuitive. Today's users have no patience for bad design, which results in an unsuccessful user experience and an unsatisfactory perception of the library.

Information Interrelationships

Librarians choose, operate, and maintain library systems and provide access to external resources, catalogs, and data sets. Providing access to this staggering variety of information resources is just one piece of a much larger puzzle. Users in the academic community, for example, require both course management tools and access to student records and registration information.

The dramatic shift in emphasis as a result of automation and the Internet has meant not only a retooling of skills for librarians and library staff, but also a similar restructuring for information providers. Companies with detailed development plans that allowed them to plan three to five years ahead for major hardware acquisition and software development now must revise their strategies. The same holds true for academic computing centers. Since the mid-1990s, the growth of the Web has brought major changes in the way providers and the acquirers of information do business. Organizations have suddenly been faced with new challenges as new ways of creating, processing, and distributing data became not only possible but required. Moreover, new markets opened and new pricing models have evolved.

Consequently, libraries have been forced to make changes to the services they offer and to the way they acquire and manage resources. Everything moves more quickly, issues are often less well-defined, and the users' demands are more immediate—especially within an undergraduate population that has never known a world without personal digital assistants and wireless communication. Is the inventor of the remote control to blame for the fact that so many users have miniscule attention spans? Users expect instant gratification, which is generating a new perception of library service.

In addition to the needs of on-site users, librarians must now consider the needs of users who work outside the library. The future of library services will be based on the development of personalized tools that foster collaboration and bring people together both inside and outside the organization. People work in new types of groups and have different expectations about communication, discovery, and retrieval tools. Students request group work space within the framework of the institution's offerings. Course material must be centrally located and accessible in a repository together with e-reserves. Faculty also need virtual workspace as they engage in collaborative research with colleagues, whether at the same institution or at other institutions, whether in academe or in the corporate world. Whatever their needs, all consumers want to be able to personalize their work areas.

The type of collaboration and personalization that many users now seek goes well beyond what most libraries presently offer. Some products on the market offer personal "my space," but these are often limited to the ILS environment and do not extend to the wider community. As vendors consider the future implications of these requirements from a development perspective, librarians speculate how they will fit such new tools into their environment.

Within the last decade, e-resources have evolved to such an extent that they now consume an ever-increasing portion of a library's budget and they resist contained or easily managed patterns of acquisition and use. How can librarians manage this growth? for libraries to remain viable, librarians must confront the situation head-on, ever mindful of the need for excellent service and speedy delivery of information to both the novice and the sophisticated information user. The skills needed by librarians today differ greatly from the skills needed by staff a decade ago—technology empowers users, whose needs and desires continually expand. Librarians must learn to take advantage of technology—even as their budgets are shrinking—in order to meet users' expectations.

The User Interface

The online public access catalog (OPAC) is often the average user's first inter-action with electronic resources. It is vital that this first encounter be positive — data in this remote-control environment should be no more than three clicks away. A good user interface, which is essential, delivers results and offers seam-less movement between systems.

The basic requirements of a good user interface include:

- excellent search capabilities;
- logical order for presentation of results;
- easy links from one resource to another;
- transparent user authentication; and
- standards-based searching.

Beyond the technical questions that are raised when considering ERM, sev-eral fundamental considerations must also be addressed:

- What will the search structures be?
- What will the search engine be?
- Will a specialty or commercial search company provide services beyond those offered by ILS vendors?[1]

In planning the user interface for electronic resources, it is important to keep in mind the ubiquitous nature of Google. Librarians love to hate Google, but it must be acknowledged that Google gets the job done for most basic searches. Paid results placement and the link popularity controversy aside, users love the fact that Google offers the instant gratification of quick answers. Users seek simplicity, and what could be simpler than a white screen with one search box?

The Support Interface

An effective ERM system requires more than a sophisticated user interface. It also requires a wide range of support services that have their roots in what has traditionally been known as technical services. These services, including acqui-sitions, serials control, and cataloging, are being modified to handle electronic resources and to accommodate new requirements and data sets. Many libraries are also responsible for supporting the Web environment.

As libraries begin to understand the need for a management system designed especially for electronic resources, some basic issues must be addressed:

- Is there sufficient staff to handle the management workload?
- Is technical expertise available?
- Is there a budget for development?
- Should the management of e-resources be handled in-house or by outside contractor?
- What sort of user interface is needed?
- Will ongoing maintenance be the responsibility of the library?
- What ERM options will provide the best control over the collection?
- How much customization is possible if the library opts to acquire a management package from a third party?

All decisions made about electronic resources should take the idea of increasing user satisfaction into account. This very complex and elaborate process involves public and technical aspects as well as a strong collection development component. Decisions about which resources should be acquired or licensed must be made. Access to a variety of resources must be consistently managed—different types of resources may require different search capabilities to retain their unique and valuable characteristics. Librarians need to prioritize databases to create a metasearch list and must decide whether all the titles included in an aggregator's database are to be cataloged. If so, how will the holdings be updated? And will sufficient, meaningful statistics be provided to evaluate use and guarantee that licensing agreements are being honored? None of these points are foreign to collection-development and cataloging staff; however, the mercurial nature of e-resources and the immediacy of user demands has changed the information environment forever.

Librarians often question whether they should create in-house systems for ERM and discover that there does not seem to be one single, correct answer to this question. Each institution will have to furnish an answer based on a host of factors ranging from the size of the collection and the availability of support staff to the needs of the user community. It is important to keep in mind, however, that the total cost of ownership (TCO) is not just the bottom line on the last page of a contract. It includes the cost of staff, maintenance, and other types of overhead. The concept of TCO is becoming increasingly prevalent as funds become more and more scarce. Generally, building an ERM system in-house is not only more expensive than acquiring an off-the-shelf system, but it may also result in assigning staff new duties or even abandoning tasks before they are completed.

Metasearch and Linking

When libraries add electronic resources to their menu of options, they must also expand the user search options so that searching and retrieving is efficient and produces valuable results. The concept of metasearching is seen as an answer to e-resource organization and access because it allows users to search multiple, disparate sources, including full-text aggregator files, abstracting and indexing databases, library catalogs, Web search engines, and more, housed locally or remotely, with a single command. Metasearch (also called broadcast searching or federated searching) may be thought of as the "buckshot" approach because when the search is launched, multiple targets are hit.

In an effective electronic environment, search results should be fully integrated and linked directly to the resources. It is easy to apply uniform relevancy ranking, sorting, and taxonomies to result sets that come from a single database housed in a single location. Using the "bucket" approach, libraries have been doing this for years with library catalogs and ILS. In a search environment where multiple databases deliver results at varying speeds and composition, good relevancy ranking or sorting is more difficult to accomplish. Although technology can make the aggregation of multiple sources into a single file and post-search processing possible, it does not appear that this will be readily available in the library world in the near future because vendors tend to offer different user interfaces and methods of presenting results.

While academic libraries have struggled with creating effective metasearch capabilities, public libraries seem to have had more success at presenting metasearch options to their patrons. Their screen designs are often clean and uncluttered, navigation is intuitive, and search options appear to be relevant to the community of users.[2]

Electronic Resources Management

Librarians manage their expensive resources in varied ways, many of which have been designed locally and are not integrated with the ILS. ERM software efficiently manages digital resources and licenses to control subscription and licensing information for such resources as e-journals, abstracting and indexing databases, and full-text databases. ERM software compiles information about all electronic resources and their licenses in one place and displays this information either by resource or by title. One ILS vendor, Innovative Interfaces, offers ERM software and four other vendors have announced their intent to develop ERM modules. These vendors have recognized that managing electronic resources is a natural extension of the other management tasks that online ILS perform.

Beyond the ILS

Libraries are being asked to provide information to an evermore assertive user population, and as a result, the library needs to be involved with designing, developing, and maintaining the services that satisfy the information needs of that population. However, there appears to be a gap in portal functionality, which means that there is a disconnect between those services commonly offered by libraries and users' desire for new and emerging tools that allow them to personalize their work. The library is well-positioned to offer services of this nature, yet none of the traditional library services vendors has developed a comprehensive tool to manage content in this fashion.

Libraries have experience in managing information and some are actively involved with institutional efforts to build disciplinary or institutional repositories. Institutional repositories take on different forms in each institution—some are generic, some are discipline-based. Regardless of the nature of the repository, librarians will require standards-based searching, results display, and retrieval so that repositories can be implemented more smoothly and have relationships to one another. There is no doubt that libraries will want to expand repositories beyond a simple silo of documents and will desire a high level of integration with the OPAC and e-resources.

The repository might provide personal, secure workspace where information can be stored and shared and is readily accessible. As with ERM software, some libraries are choosing such complex tools as D-Space or Fedora to build their repositories, and some will look to their library services or ILS vendor to bridge the gap.

Libraries are creeping, or perhaps ricocheting, past the confines of traditional library systems, applications, and expectations. It behooves everyone in the information services industry—librarians and vendors alike—to pay very close attention to this trend.

To do that, librarians must stay in step with larger institutional goals and objectives. This need not be complicated; it may be as simple as providing a link from the library's home page to related campus sites.

In some respects, the situation libraries face today is reminiscent of the issues that were addressed when retrospective conversion of bibliographic records was a major concern. At that time, decisions had to be made not only about which collections and records to convert, but which to convert first. Usually the easiest and least complex records received the highest priority for conversion, while the more difficult or complicated records were converted last. In today's electronic environment, similar choices must be made. As libraries migrate from printed sources to online resources, how will they meet diverse user demands for relevant and speedy access to information? Could libraries implement simple solutions for controlling e-resources first and leave more complex solutions for later, with the expectation that as technology is developed and tested, control of resources will be easier?

Conclusion

Librarians face new challenges daily. Information providers, subscription agents, serials data providers, publishers, and ILS vendors all confront similar challenges. Everyone must adapt to survive and such new tools as ERM software and turnkey institutional repositories will aid this adaptation. Ongoing ERM problems must be faced and solved. Keeping track of data sources and making decisions about whether to renew them or not is in itself a major task, but one where a growing number of solutions are now within reach.

REFERENCE NOTES

1. Two examples of specialty or commercial search companies are FAST (www .fastsearch.com) and Northern Light (www.northernlight.com). Accessed 16 April 2005.

2. For a good example of a public library Web site, see Westerville Public Library, "MetaFind: Universal Search Interface" (Westerville, Ohio: WPL, 2005). Accessed 16 April 2005, http://catalog.westervillelibrary.org/.

Electronic Resource Management Systems
What Should They Do?

TIMOTHY D. JEWELL

Recent expenditure trend data from the Association of Research Libraries (ARL) shows that spending by research libraries for electronic resources has grown much more rapidly than materials budgets and that libraries are shifting toward reliance on electronic resources.[1] This dependence has intensified within the last year or two as libraries shed paper journal subscriptions to help pay for online access.

User behavior and attitudes have changed even more quickly. For example, nearly half of the undergraduates surveyed by Outsell and the Digital Library Federation (DLF) for their study of the scholarly information environment indicated that they use electronic resources either exclusively or almost exclusively.[2] The same study showed that many faculty and graduate students would like to see more journals available electronically, and that users now expect their libraries' services to be comparable in power and convenience to the popular Google Web search engine and Web sites such as Amazon.com.

These developments provide the context for what many librarians find to be an increasingly complex, multidimensional, and daunting challenge: successfully managing their collections of electronic resources. A study of Digital Library Federation member practices, related to the acquisition and use of electronic resources, identifies and describes some noteworthy trends.[3] As these libraries acquired more bibliographic databases, they had to address the fundamental electronic resource management (ERM) problem of describing and effectively presenting information about these resources. Newer resources, such as aggregator databases from companies like EBSCO, Gale, LexisNexis, and

This paper is an abridged and otherwise modified version of parts of the report of the DLF ERMI (www.diglib.org/pubs/dlfermi0408/). Readers interested in additional detail can find it in that publication.

ProQuest, which provide access to the contents or partial contents of large numbers of periodicals, pose a related challenge. Although such collections often provide substantial benefits, reliably and routinely determining and describing the journals they provide—indicating for what periods of time, in what format, and with what degree of currency or completeness—has proven to be an elusive goal. The growth of electronic journals and databases has added to this problem while it complicated and transformed the processes associated with acquiring and servicing library materials.

Many libraries present users with special alphabetical or subject lists of electronic resources and journals, including the contents of aggregator databases and e-journal packages. Companies including Serials Solutions, TDNet, and EBSCO offer various services aimed at supporting these sorts of functions. In recent years libraries have linked their indexing and full-text resources through proprietary database vendor solutions and broader, standards-based tools like ExLibris's SFX—thus adding another layer of complexity to the management of electronic resources.

Other changes that are much less visible to users have also been taking place. As electronic resources have become pervasive, formal license agreements have come to supplement or supersede copyright law as the basis for defining and determining their appropriate use. Despite the welcome and promising appearance of model licenses and other efforts to standardize license terms, libraries continue to invest substantial time and effort reviewing and negotiating license terms.[4] License negotiations may become complex and protracted, involving staff at multiple levels of both licensor and licensee organizations. As a result, some libraries make special efforts to track the status of a particular negotiation and to describe and present important license terms to users and staff.

At the same time, libraries have been entering into complex consortium-based purchasing arrangements characterized by ongoing financial commitments and new communication, evaluation, and decision-making processes. Once acquired, these same resources must also be supported through specialized skills and with new kinds of information. A defining facet of the new electronic environment is that staff from disparate units of larger libraries have begun playing new and important specialized roles within the complex processes of selection, support, and evaluation of electronic resources. Most of these staff need a wide range of specialized information. For example, staff members in different areas may need to know the status of a resource within the local acquisition and licensing process. Others may need to know access details, whether access problems related to a particular resource have arisen and who was involved in what specific troubleshooting actions. Several libraries have also implemented planned, cyclical reviews of their electronic resources, and—with that in mind—systematically gather and report all available information on their use.

The critical finding from the 2001 DLF study was that a number of libraries found their existing integrated library system (ILS) incapable of supporting functions crucial to ERM, and had begun to design and build local automated tools to fill these serious gaps in functionality. The goal of this article is to sketch the functionality built into some of these systems and summarize a set of functional requirements incorporated into the report of the DLF Electronic Resource Management Initiative (ERMI).[5]

Current Efforts to Create ERM Systems

As work on the 2001 DLF study progressed, librarians who shared an interest in finding effective ERM systems were contacted. As a result Jewell and Adam Chandler of Cornell University established a Web site for exchanging information about local systems and fostering communication among interested librarians.[6] Once they identified local systems, they asked librarians about the functions and data elements of these systems and they made the information available through the site, titled Web Hub. These functions and data elements were analyzed and summarized for the DLF report.[7] Within a year or two of the study, some twenty libraries and library-based organizations announced that they had produced or were planning to produce such systems. See table 1.

Each system reflects specific local requirements and development constraints, and many exhibit creative and noteworthy features. Penn State University Libraries' Electronic Resources Licensing and Information Center (ERLIC), developed in 1999, was designed to address a fairly limited need, but has since been expanded substantially. Initially developed using Microsoft Access to track

TABLE 1 |
| Libraries and Organizations with Library-based ERM Initiatives

California Digital Library	Tri-College Consortium (Haverford, Bryn Mawr, Swarthmore)
Colorado Alliance of Research Libraries (Gold Rush)	
	UCLA
Columbia University	University of Georgia
Griffith University (Australia)	University of Michigan
Harvard University	University of Minnesota
Johns Hopkins University (HERMES)	University of Notre Dame
MIT (VERA)	University of Texas (License Tracker)
North Carolina State University	University of Virginia
Penn State University (ERLIC)	Willamette University
Stanford University	Yale University

the status of orders and anticipate renewals, ERLIC and its successor, ERLIC2 (a ColdFusion Web database) have evolved into centralized sources of ordering, access, authentication, and licensing information.[8] The MIT Libraries' Virtual Electronic Resource Access (VERA) system also exhibits a spectrum of functions and incorporates both extensive support for back-office staff functions and requirements and numerous noteworthy public Web page design features.[9] Yale's schematized public presentation of license terms serves as an interesting supplement to MIT's approach to the same problem.

Like ERLIC and VERA, UCLA's Electronic Resources Database (ERDb) system was developed to address a wide range of functionality. That functionality and its screen designs are of substantial interest, but related working documents also articulate the following useful guidelines for development of an ERM system:

- accommodate growth
- design for flexibility
- create one database with many views
- avoid unnecessary duplication
- implement in phases[10]

Similarly broad in scope is Johns Hopkins's HERMES, which is based on PostgreSQL and ColdFusion, and is now available on an open-source basis.[11] While intended to dynamically generate public Web pages, HERMES carefully analyzes staff roles, workflows, and associated functional requirements, which makes it especially interesting. Also worthy of mention is Gold Rush, developed by the Colorado Alliance of Research Libraries.[12] Gold Rush was the first system available for sale that incorporated substantial functionality for e-resource subscription management. Reasonably priced and offering support for both individual libraries and library consortia, Gold Rush enables a central consortium administrator to push out to member libraries a record with a range of information pertaining to an electronic resource.

Functions and Examples

A Life-cycle based Overview

Effective ERM is similar to records management in that they both depend on the execution of a wide range of functions. Records management has been defined as the "systematic control of all organizational records during the various stages of their lifecycle: from their creation or receipt, through their processing, distribution, maintenance and use, to their ultimate disposition."[13] Although it is not necessary for libraries to create licensed electronic resources in the current environment, they need to evaluate new products and services. There are other parallels between a simplified records management and ERM life-cycle models.

Based on the functions and reports available through the HERMES system, staff users at Johns Hopkins play five different roles: selector, superselector, acquisitions administrator, library systems administrator, and public display administrator.[14]

PRODUCT CONSIDERATION AND TRIAL PROCESS

The selector identifies a resource, determines whether a trial is necessary, and gathers preliminary license information. The acquisitions administrator negotiates a trial license if one is needed. Following a trial, the selector recommends approval or disapproval of the purchase, which the superselector then determines. Trial URLs, passwords, and publicity are also established and recorded during this phase.

ACQUISITION PROCESS

This phase involves three more or less distinct subprocesses, which may take place in parallel with one another. The acquisitions administrator negotiates the license and enters related information into HERMES while the computing services administrator determines technical feasibility and gives or withholds permission to proceed. Remaining tasks, also the responsibility of the acquisitions administrator, relate to funding and actual purchase.

IMPLEMENTATION

During this phase, staff work out and record authentication details, conduct any necessary database configuration work, and catalog and incorporate the resource and related components into public Web pages. Descriptive tasks can be difficult and time consuming at this stage—particularly if the resource in question is an e-journal or aggregator package that contains large numbers of journals or other content. In addition, public Web pages can be presented in a number of ways and can include the information about licensing terms for staff and end users. It may also be necessary to make the resource recognizable to a link resolver or proxy server.

PRODUCT MAINTENANCE AND REVIEW

One of many important clusters of tasks within this phase is subscription renewal, which can be triggered by date-configurable reminders to staff and could involve price or license-term renegotiation. Holdings (coverage) information encountered during the implementation phase must be maintained. Acquiring and making usage data available to staff and identifying and resolving access problems and other technical issues can affect the renewal process.

Sample Product Consideration and Trial Process Screens

The preceding inventory of life-cycle tasks and roles may not correspond closely with the screen displays that staff actually see when using an ERM system or a derivative. For example, the functions could be reorganized and presented according to staff role—as they are within the HERMES system. This underscores the relevance and value of UCLA's ERDb design principle—one database, many views. Figure 1 is an example of multiple views and is another way to organize similar information.

In figure 1, information from different life-cycle phases, such as acquisition (purchase order number and vendor), implementation (URL, location), and product maintenance and review (renewal date, technical support contact, information about usage data) is presented together—presumably because the various staff members using this screen all need to see the information it contains.

In figure 2, the ERDb system's resource screen includes information relevant to a couple of e-resource life-cycle phases. In addition to basic identifying or descriptive information that will be used throughout the resource life-cycle, selection information, such as sponsoring unit and selector, are available as well as acquisitions information, such as vendor and purchase order number.

The ERDb screen in figure 3 identifies the licensor and UCLA's negotiator, contains a link to a redacted version of the license, and provides space for a detailed analysis of the specific rights and other details included in the license.

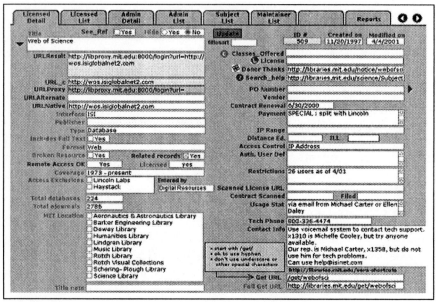

FIGURE 1

MIT Libraries VERA Staff Display Showing Range of Functions (reprinted with permission of MIT Libraries)

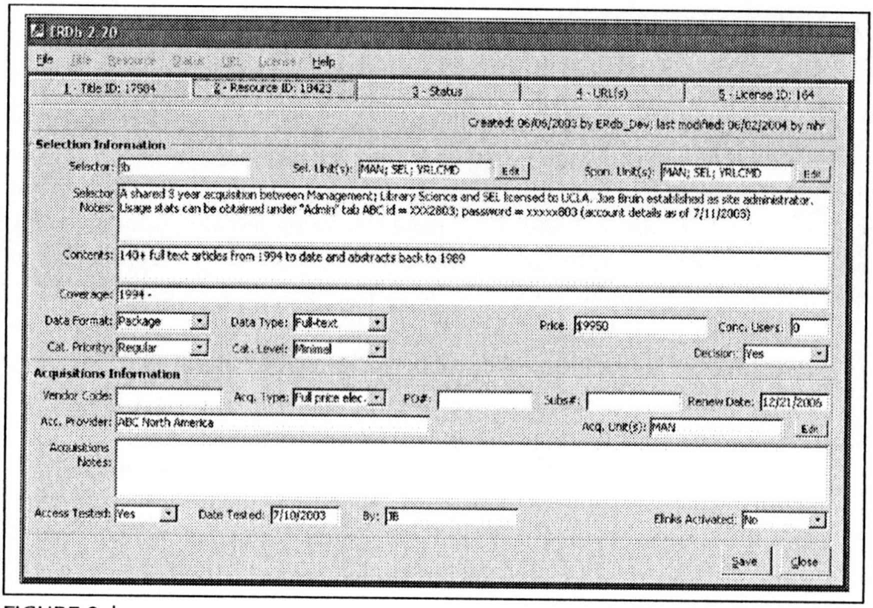

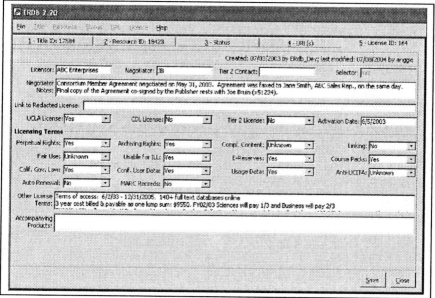

FIGURE 2

UCLA Libraries ERDb Resource Screen (reprinted with permission of UCLA Library)

FIGURE 3

UCLA Libraries ERDb License Screen (reprinted with permission of UCLA Library)

Implementation Processes and Public Web Pages: Alphabetical and Subject Presentations

Libraries commonly present users with multiple routes to licensed resources—including OPAC entries, alphabetical and subject Web page listings, e-reserve links, and links connecting index or abstract entries to the corresponding full text. However, the mechanisms that provide these presentations are generally hidden from public view. Figure 4 shows what users at UCLA encounter when they follow a link from the libraries' gateway page to online materials.

UCLA, like many libraries, distinguishes between electronic journals and article databases. Those distinctions need to be made within their database. Alphabetical and subject presentations used by UCLA are like those of many other libraries. See figures 5 and 6.

Helping to drive and support these presentations is information gathered and maintained through the ERDb title view, such as the basic bibliographic data for the resource. See figure 7. Another view relates the component titles of an e-journal package to a parent record, which is necessary for a number of functions, such as linking license terms to particular titles. The title view also associates a resource with both subjects and types of resources. See figures 8 and 9.

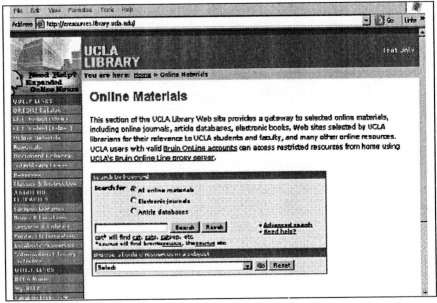

FIGURE 4 | UCLA Online Materials Web Page (reprinted with permission of UCLA Library)

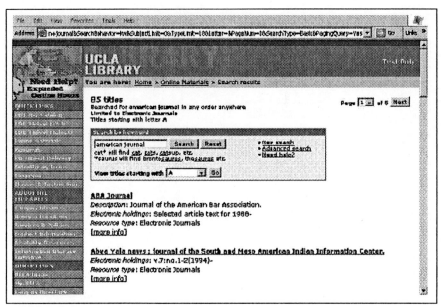

FIGURE 5

UCLA Online Materials Web Page Title List (reprinted with permission of UCLA Library)

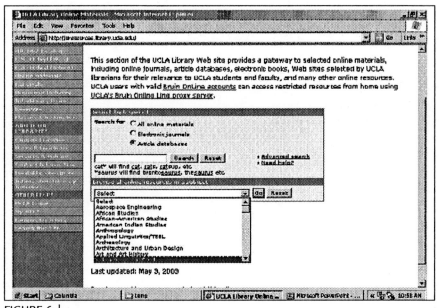

FIGURE 6

UCLA Online Materials Web Page Showing Drop-down Subject List (reprinted with permission of UCLA Library)

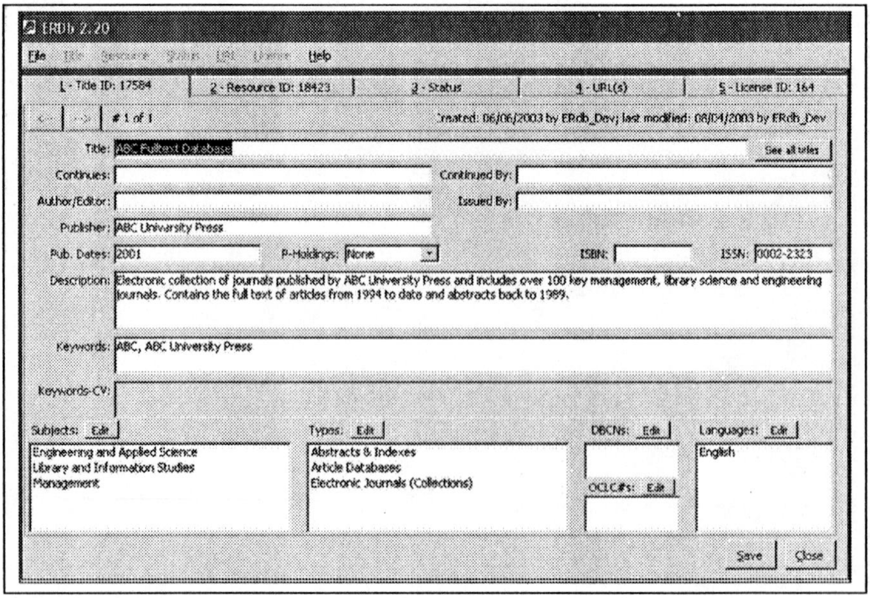

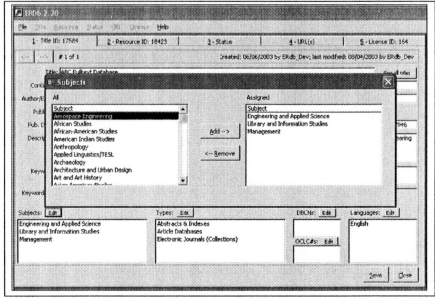

FIGURE 7
UCLA ERDb Title Screen (reprinted with permission of UCLA Library)

FIGURE 8
UCLA ERDb Title Screen Showing Drop-down Subject List (reprinted with permission of UCLA Library)

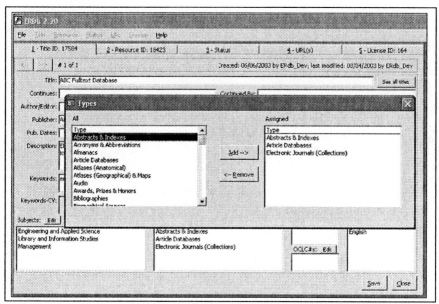

FIGURE 9

UCLA ERDb Title Screen Showing Drop-down Resource Type List (reprinted with permission of UCLA Library)

Public Web Pages: Extended Information

Like ERDb, MIT's VERA generates subject and alphabetical Web pages for both databases and e-journals. See figures 10 and 11. VERA also describes e-resource availability by specific location and manages and generates resource-specific URLs.

That VERA incorporates and presents a wide range of information using special-purpose icons is especially noteworthy. In figure 11, the "Go" button indicates that a resource is available to the MIT community from off-campus, the "?" icon leads to search tips and other documentation, and the "C" icon leads to information about upcoming classes on using the specific resource. The international "NOT" symbol also indicates resource-specific access problems. Of even greater interest is the way in which VERA incorporates license information. In addition to the generic message about appropriate and inappropriate use of resources that precedes the resource list, the "L" icon indicates when more specific license-related information is available. For example, in figure 12 the "L" icon associated with the entry for *Abstracts of the Papers Communicated to the Royal Society of London* leads the user to a summary of key provisions of the JSTOR license that governs its use.

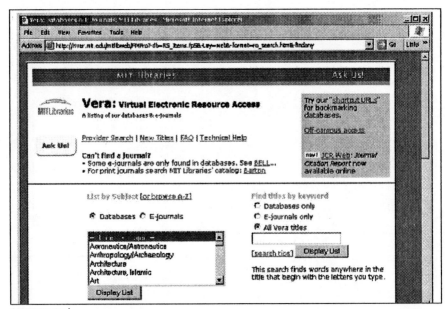

FIGURE 10

MIT Libraries VERA Subject Listing of Electronic Resources
(reprinted with permission of MIT Libraries)

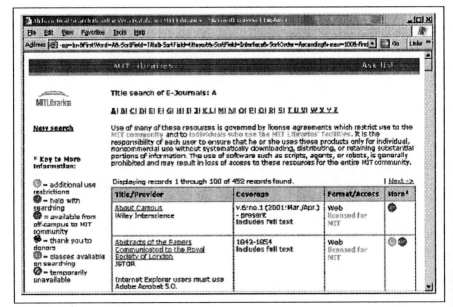

FIGURE 11

MIT Libraries VERA Alphabetical Display Showing E-resource Details
Provided and Key to More Information (reprinted with permission
of MIT Libraries)

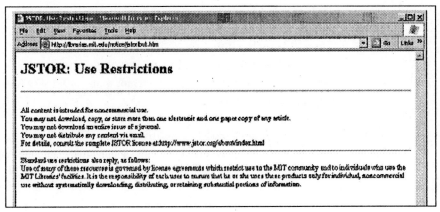

FIGURE 12 | MIT Libraries VERA System Summary of JSTOR Use Restrictions (reprinted with permission of MIT Libraries)

Yale University Libraries' public e-resource pages integrate instructional and licensing information in clear and understandable ways. For example, figure 13 shows an alphabetical listing of databases in the social sciences, including Academic Universe.

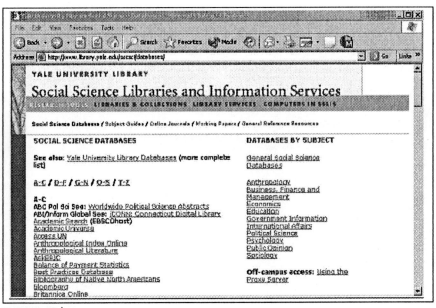

FIGURE 13 | Yale University Libraries Social Science E-resource Subject List Entry for Academic Universe (reprinted with permission of the Yale University Library)

When users click on the Academic Universe entry, they are taken to the display of additional information shown in figure 14, which includes a group of "Help" tools as well as a link to "Permitted Uses of Databases."

The link to permitted uses of databases takes users to the appropriate section of a lengthy document summarizing permitted uses for many or most of the library's licensed resources. See figure 15.

This presentation is noteworthy for a few reasons. First, the licensing agreement for each resource has been analyzed to determine provisions in eight key areas, with a simple yes or no to indicate whether or not a particular use is permitted. Second, the summary grid provides space to expand any of the key terms if needed. Lastly, the full terms and conditions of the agreement can be accessed from this screen. In this case, the link takes users to the LexisNexis Web page, but it could just as easily take them to a locally-digitized version of an institution-specific license. See figure 16.

The terms of use section from the Colorado Alliance of Research Libraries's Gold Rush Staff Toolbox serves as an interesting contrast to the presentations of the MIT and Yale license information. Where the MIT and Yale summaries are designed for use by those library systems, Gold Rush can be used to provide summary license terms to all libraries sharing the system and particular resources. See figure 17.

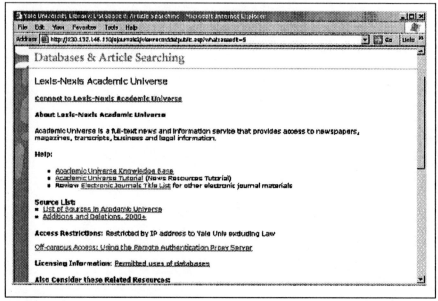

FIGURE 14

Yale University Libraries E-resource List Entry for LexisNexis Academic Universe (reprinted with permission of the Yale University Library)

LexisNexis Academic & Library Services
    Academic UNIVerse
    Congressional Universe
    Statistical Universe
    <div align="center">**Licensing Information**</div>		

Yes	Copy	General Terms and Conditions for Use of the LexisNexis Services
Yes	Download	
No	ILL	
No	ILL (Partial)	
Yes	Limited sharing for scholarly purposes	
Yes	Course & Reserve Packs	
Yes	Print	
Yes	Use by Walk-ins	For educational use only; May not actively promote walk-in use.

FIGURE 15

Yale University Libraries License Information Summary for LexisNexis Academic Universe (reprinted with permission of the Yale University Library)

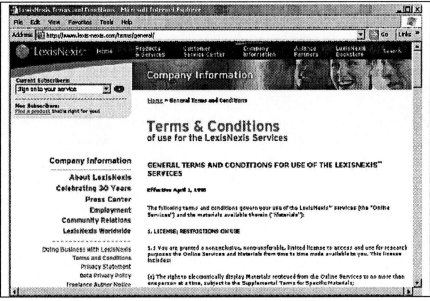

FIGURE 16

LexisNexis Academic Terms and Conditions Page (reprinted with permission of LexisNexis Academic & Library Solutions)

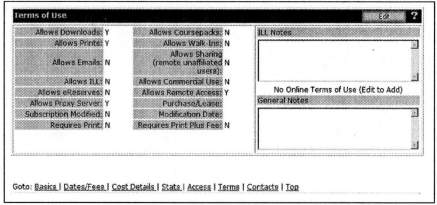

FIGURE 17

Terms of Use Area from Colorado Alliance's Gold Rush Staff Toolbox
(reprinted with permission of the Colorado Alliance of Research Libraries)

Product Maintenance and Review Screens

Once access to a product has been established and its availability made known,
any number of problems may occur. For example, a vendor or other information provider may need to take a product offline for planned maintenance or to
address technical difficulties that suddenly emerge. Occasionally vendor files of
a subscriber's IP addresses may fail to reflect recent changes or become corrupt
and access to services will be affected or delays in invoicing and payment can
result in outages. These problems may manifest themselves in a variety of ways,
but what may be more vexing to staff and users is the fact that an access problem related to a package of electronic journals or an aggregator service can
affect all the component journals in the package—for which entries may be dis-
persed throughout an online catalog or online Web list of available journals.

When any of these circumstances arise, it may be difficult or even impossible to communicate the information to appropriate staff and affected users. One
promising approach for facilitating communication is ERDb's status screen.
See figure 18. The upper half of this screen displays basic information about the
resource in question, while the lower half provides space to record information
about a reported incident, such as a user's name, IP address, Internet service
provider, browser, description of the problem, action required, and status of the
problem.

Another approach to communicating open problems is allowing either
users or staff to quickly identify any resources to which access was likely to be a
problem at a particular time. See figure 19.

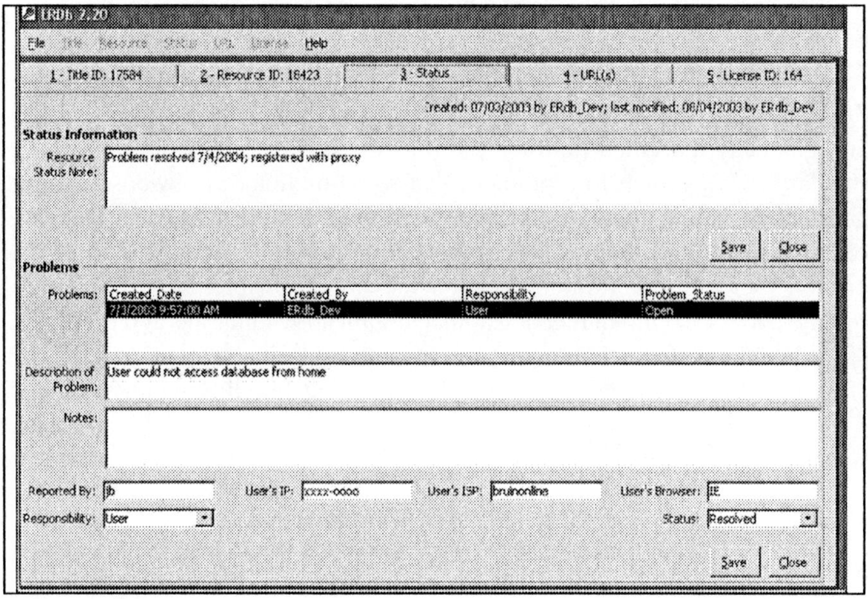

FIGURE 18 | UCLA Libraries ERDb Status Screen (reprinted with permission of the UCLA Library)

Electronic Resources Licensing & Information Center (ERLIC2)

Today's Billboard:

5/28/02	Elsevier	Access (V)	Access problem with selected Elsevier titles; Serials Dept working to resolve
5/27/02	ERDS	Trial	New Database Trial "ERDS"
5/26/02	E-Journal List	Access (L)	TECH working on Cold Fusion Server problem, e-journal list not working more . . .

FIGURE 19 | Penn State University Libraries ERLIC System Prototype of E-resource Billboard Function (reprinted with permission of Penn State University Libraries)

Toward a Generalized Solution: DLF ERMI

As systems were identified and listed on Web Hub, an effort was made to capture information about the specific functions and data elements of each system and gradually it seemed not only possible and but also desirable to pursue a standardized approach to a problem that so many libraries obviously shared. This notion gained momentum when the ALCTS Technical Services Directors of Large Research Libraries Discussion Group began to sponsor informal discussion sessions at ALA Annual Conferences and Midwinter Meetings starting in June 2001. That initial meeting attracted some forty librarians and eventually led to additional discussions about functionality and data elements and the creation of an informal steering group that included Jewell, Chandler, Sharon Farb, and Angela Riggio from UCLA; Nathan Robertson from Johns Hopkins; Ivy Anderson from Harvard; and Kimberly Parker from Yale.

This group worked with Patricia Harris and Priscilla Caplan at NISO and Daniel Greenstein (at that time director of DLF) to begin serious discussions of possible standards which ultimately led to the Workshop on Standards for Electronic Resource Management in May 2002.[15] The workshop was attended by approximately fifty librarians and representatives from a number of vendors and publishers, including EBSCO, Endeavor, ExLibris, Fretwell-Downing, Innovative Interfaces, Sirsi, and Serials Solutions. In addition to presentations and discussions concerning the nature and extent of the ERM problem, a proposed entity relationship diagram (ERD) and several lists of data elements were presented and discussed. One important outcome was a consensus that standards to help guide the development of ERM systems were desirable. Consequently, the steering group decided to consider a more formal, collaborative approach to establishing related best practices and standards. Such an effort might reduce unnecessary costs and duplication at the institutional level, support interoperability and data sharing among diverse systems and organizations, and provide extended benefits to the wider library community.

With these benefits in mind, the steering group submitted a proposal to launch ERMI, which was accepted by DLF in October 2002. The most important aim of the project has been fostering the rapid development of systems and tools for managing electronic resources—whether by individual libraries, consortia, or vendors. A series of interrelated documents upon which libraries and vendors could base their efforts was proposed and recently completed, including a road map, workflow diagrams, a revised ERD, and an extended list of data elements and definitions. To provide for ongoing expert advice, two reactor panels (advisory groups) were formed. The librarian reactor panel consisted of librarians deemed specially qualified by their experience and interest in ERM systems to provide the necessary feedback. The vendor reactor panel was made up of representatives of ILS and other companies serving the library market.

The importance and potential value of standards to ERM systems was considered fundamental to the initiative because standards could play an important role in reducing vendor development costs and risks—thus accelerating the development process. In addition, although ERM systems might be developed and marketed as standalone systems, it seems likely that these systems would have to be overlaid on or otherwise linked to other existing tools, such as serials or acquisitions systems, online catalogs, and e-resource gateways.[16] It was therefore seen as critical to establish predictable pathways among variant data streams. Libraries that have developed their own systems, or wish to do so in the short term, might ultimately hope to transfer their data to a vendor system. If agreement on standards could be reached, those libraries could develop, modify, or align their systems with the standards—thus paving the way toward data and system migration. Lastly, it is conceivable—given standard ways of doing so—that libraries could exchange license information with trading partners or create systems that would describe the availability of specific electronic sources for such uses as interlibrary loan.

In spring 2003, staff from the Harvard and MIT libraries met with staff from library system vendor Ex Libris to discuss possible work on an ERM tool. While lists of data elements from the initiative were available and were discussed, attention quickly turned to the obvious question: "What is the functionality?" To answer that question, Harvard and MIT staff—led by steering group member Ivy Anderson and MIT's Ellen Duranceau—collaborated on a description of the functionality needed in an ERM system. The document was subsequently broadened and made more generic and its function is described as follows:

> This document was intended to clearly and comprehensively identify the functions that an ERM system would serve. Libraries could use it to support a discussion of the most important features they might wish to purchase or incorporate into a locally developed electronic resource management system, or use the specifications as an early draft vendor RFP for such a system.[17]

The functional requirements identify and describe the tasks needed to support electronic resources throughout their life cycles, including selection and acquisition, access provision, resource administration, staff and end-user support, and renewal and retention decisions. They are based on a set of guiding principles that can be summarized as follows:

- Print and e-resource management and access should be through an integrated environment

- Information provided to the user should be consistent, regardless of the path taken
- There should be a single point of maintenance for each data element
- ERM systems should be flexible enough for new or additional fields and data elements to be added easily

In addition, a few core requirements for ERM systems were identified:

- Represent the relationships among individual e-resources, packages, licenses, and online interfaces
- Associate the characteristics of a given license, interface, or package with the resources to which it applies
- Provide robust reporting and data export capabilities

The final document contains forty-seven requirements—more than half of which deal with functionality needed to support staff activities. The scope of the requirements can be seen in this summary:

> *General* (four requirements). These include the three core requirements in more precise language, and state that "security features to control staff views and maintenance rights" are also required.
>
> *Resource Discovery* (seven requirements). This group addresses the need to make resources available through or pass information about them to OPACs and Web presentation services, and for contextual presentation of license information at the point of access.
>
> *Bibliographic Management* (two requirements). These requirements address the need for a single point of data entry and maintenance for bibliographic information and the ability to import aggregator holdings and subscription management data.
>
> *Access Management* (five requirements). This grouping covers the management of basic access-related information, such as uniform resource identifiers (URIs), user IDs and passwords, and lists of institutional IP addresses as well as the requirement to interoperate with or submit data to related technical systems, such as proxy servers and persistent naming services.
>
> *Staff Requirements* (twenty-nine requirements)
>
>> *General Interface Requirements* (four requirements). The staff interface should be organized into views that are optimized for particular areas of staff activity or interest, such as resource acquisition, troubleshooting, license management, or administration and statistics.

Selection and Evaluation Processes (nine requirements). An ERM system should support the recording of actions and other information at various steps in what may be decentralized processes, and have the capability to perform specified actions or to send alerts in defined circumstances. Actions and triggers should be customizable by the library to support a site-specific workflow.

Resource Administration and Management (eleven requirements). This group describes functionality related to administrative usernames and passwords, local configuration options, hardware and software requirements, and troubleshooting support, the ability to flag resources as unavailable, and the ability to store information about available usage data.

Business Functions (five requirements). This grouping covers pricing models, cancellation restrictions, renewal and termination activities, cost-sharing, and consortial relationship information.

To help make the functional requirements as generic or universal as possible, they were reviewed and discussed with members of the librarian reactor panel, who were asked to distinguish between the requirements they saw as core or essential and those they felt were nonessential. It was gratifying to the steering group (although dismaying, perhaps, to vendors) that every requirement was considered core by at least one member of the reactor panel.

One of the functions that the librarians viewed as most important was the ability to manage the relationships among bibliographic entities (i.e., individual titles) and the packages, licenses, and interfaces through which they are made available. Another function that was considered essential was the ability to store access-related information, such as URLs, user IDs and passwords, and institutional IP addresses. The ability to record authorized user categories and other license permissions, restrictions, and metadata about the agreement itself was deemed equally important. Not surprisingly, the ability to store license permissions and associated metadata was one of the most frequently cited requirements, and the ability to link to an online version of a redacted license was also desired by most. Offering a single point of maintenance for bibliographic and other descriptive data, and facilitating electronic transfer of holdings and other subscription data from external providers was also identified as essential, as was supporting institutional workflows through customized routing and notification tools.

Other core or essential features included the ability to store information about administrative IDs and passwords and information about and access to usage statistics.

Several important themes also emerged in the reactor panel discussions:

Most libraries want to be able to use their existing ILS for core acquisitions functions, such as ordering, budgeting, and fund accounting. However, these systems must be enhanced to accommodate the additional functionality required by e-resources. If ERM is implemented in a standalone application, libraries will generally choose to continue to perform core acquisitions activities in their ILS, but may want to export some data to the ERM system for analysis and reporting.

The relationship of the descriptive data in an ERM to other descriptive systems, such as the OPAC, federated search tools, and link-resolution services, is of concern to many libraries. All agreed that minimizing duplicative data and enabling these systems to talk to one another was important. As one reactor said, the OPAC should be recognized as the home of MARC bibliographic data.

Usage statistics are an increasing focus of interest for many libraries. In addition to relying on vendor-provided usage data, quite a few libraries also collect such data locally. The members of the reactor panel were asked whether ERM systems should store usage data or merely point users to external data sources. Although most found pointers to be adequate, a number of group members felt that a common framework for storing and presenting statistics from disparate sources should be provided.

Persistent URIs are used by many but not all larger libraries. Where they are used, support for them can be critical to the library's operation. In general, libraries that assign persistent URIs want to be able to record them in the ERM system, and many agreed that being able to generate persistent URIs was both desirable and feasible because the algorithms by which they are assigned tend to be highly formulaic.

Toward the Future of E-resource Management

The main reason behind the development of DLF ERMI was the realization that few libraries had the tools needed to successfully manage electronic resources and that developing them would be difficult, time consuming, and complex. From the beginning, the members of the ERMI steering group felt that solving such a large and important problem would require extensive collaboration and investment. It is consequently very satisfying to report that librarians and vendors have invariably been very positive in their reactions to the initiative.

Most importantly at the time, a number of ILS vendors had begun developing ERM systems or services or had announced plans to do so; most of this work has drawn heavily from the project's draft functional requirements and data elements.

As important as these efforts are, their long-term success is uncertain unless work to develop relevant data standards takes place at the same time. Fortunately, work toward resolution of some critical standards-related problems—such as descriptions of serial holdings—seems well underway. The resolution of other important problems will probably take longer. For example, the steering committee concluded during its work that it would be desirable to establish a single global e-resource identification system or registry for packages, providers, and interfaces, but that doing so might require a separate initiative.

Issues related to standardized communication about intellectual property, licensing, and permitted use will also probably require considerably more additional time and work. Luckily, there is evidence of interest in this problem. For example, discussions at the 2004 Cooperative Online Serials' (CONSER) Summit on Serials in the Digital Environment suggested that some publishers may be ready to experiment with providing public versions of their licenses to libraries. There was interest in the idea of establishing a testbed of licenses marked up in extensible markup language (XML) for importing into local ERM systems.[18] There have also been some discussions about establishing a standard data dictionary for publisher licensing and rights expression, using the ERMI data dictionary as a starting point.

Perhaps just as challenging is the question of whether stand-alone ERM applications capable of being integrated into ILS can be developed. In addition to efforts to standardize data elements, Visionary Technology in Library Solutions, a new initiative aimed at "enabling Web services between disparate applications used in libraries," may hold substantial promise in this regard.[19]

The work of the initiative has concentrated first on the needs of individual libraries rather than on the needs of library consortia. While that focus made it possible to make rapid headway in developing the initiative, a broader view that takes consortial support functions into account is highly desirable. It will be complicated by the fact that library consortia differ substantially from one another—some like OhioLINK and the California Digital Library (CDL) have significant central funding and a broad service mandate, and others function more as buying clubs with corresponding limited missions, staffing, and goals. Nevertheless, steps to address the consortial issues are being taken. For example, CDL has initiated an effort to identify its requirements for an ERM system and will be soliciting vendor proposals. Discussions of consortial administrivia and ERM were held at the International Coalition of Library Consortia (ICLC) conference in March 2004, and it is conceivable that these discussions and the

CDL ERM review process could result in development of a generic statement of consortial ERM requirements.[20]

Although there is some provision for usage data within the ERMI data model, it would be desirable to better describe both the analyses libraries will perform on the data and how such data might be passed more easily to libraries for incorporation into their ERM systems. Touchstones for such an analysis would include Project COUNTER, the ARL E-metrics initiative, and model usage data programs, such as the Data Farm developed at the University of Pennsylvania.[21]

Resolving these issues will require substantial, ongoing, organized, cooperative effort from libraries, consortia, publishers, serial agents and support companies, and library system vendors—as well as effective structures for communication. The new electronic environment in which libraries, publishers, and vendors operate has evolved quickly and has become quite complex in relatively short order, but the complexities of today could pale in comparison to what may be just around the corner—as investments in electronic resources grow, technical innovation continues, and business models evolve. No matter how the environment changes, new tools, standards, smart choices, and collaboration will be needed, and it is hoped that DLF ERM has enabled all of these to happen more quickly and effectively.

The author would like to express his deep thanks to the other members of the initiative's steering committee: Ivy Anderson, Adam Chandler, Sharon Farb, Kimberly Parker, Angela Riggio, and Nathan D. M. Robertson. This article (and the initiative) would not have been possible without their many direct and indirect contributions.

REFERENCE NOTES

1. Association of Research Libraries, "Collections and Access for the Twenty-First-Century Scholar: Changing Roles of Research Libraries," *ARL: A Bimonthly Report on Research Library Issues and Actions from ARL, CNI, and SPARC* 225 (Dec. 2002). Accessed 16 April 2005, www.arl.org/newsltr/225/index.html; Association of Research Libraries, *ARL Supplementary Statistics 2001–2002* (Washington, D.C.: ARL, 2003). Accessed 16 April 2005, www.arl.org/stats/pubpdf/sup02.pdf.

2. Amy Friedlander, *Dimensions and Use of the Scholarly Information Environment: Introduction to a Data Set Assembled by the Digital Library Federation and Outsell, Inc.* (Washington, D.C.: Digital Library Federation and Council on Library and Information Resources, 2002). Accessed 16 April 2005, www.clir.org/pubs/reports/pub110/contents.html.

3. Timothy D. Jewell, *Selection and Presentation of Commercially Available Electronic Resources*, (Washington, D.C.: Digital Library Federation and Council on Library and Information Resources, 2001). Accessed 16 April 2005, www.clir.org/pubs/reports/pub99/pub99.pdf.

4. John Cox, "Model Generic Licenses: Cooperation and Competition" *Serials Review* 26, no. 1 (2000): 3–9; Council on Library and Information Resources, *CLIR/DLF Model License* (New Haven, Conn.: Yale University Library, 2001). Accessed 16 April 2005, www.library.yale.edu/~llicense/modlic.shtml.

5. Timothy D. Jewell et al., *Electronic Resource Management: The Report of the DLF Initiative* (Washington, D.C.: Digital Library Federation, 2004). Accessed 16 April 2005, www.diglib.org/pubs/dlfermi0408/.

6. Timothy D. Jewell and Adam Chandler, "Web Hub for Developing Administrative Metadata for Electronic Resources." Accessed 16 April 2005, www.library.cornell.edu/cts/elicensestudy/home.html.

7. Jewell, *Selection and Presentation*, 26.

8. Nancy Markle Stanley, Angelina F. Holden, and Betty L. Nirnberger, "Taming the Octopus: Getting a Grip on Electronic Resources," *Serials Librarian* 38, nos. 3–4 (2000): 363–68; Robert Alan, "Keeping Track of Electronic Resources to Keep Them on Track" (PowerPoint presentation for NASIG 2002). Accessed 13 October 2005, www.library.cornell.edu/cts/elicensestudy/pennstate/PSUNASIGPresentation2002.ppt.

9. Ellen Finnie Duranceau, "License Compliance," *Serials Review* 26, no. 1 (2000): 53–58; Ellen Finnie Duranceau, "License Tracking," *Serials Review* 26, no. 3 (2000): 69–73; Nicole Hennig, "Improving Access to E-journals and Databases at the MIT Libraries: Building a Database-backed Web Site Called 'VERA,'" *Serials Librarian* 41, nos. 3–4 (2002): 227–54. Accessed 16 April 2005, www.hennigweb.com/publications/vera.html.

10. Sharon E. Farb, "UCLA Electronic Resource Database Project Overview," (PowerPoint presentation; other documentation available on Web Hub). Accessed 16 April 2005, www.library.cornell.edu/cts/elicensestudy/ucla/ALAMidwinter2002.ppt.

11. Mark Cyzyk and Nathan D. M. Robertson, "HERMES: The Hopkins Electronic Resource Management System," *Information Technology and Libraries* 22, no. 3 (2001): 12–17.

12. Melissa Stockton and George Machovec, "Gold Rush: A Digital Registry of Electronic Journals," *Technical Services Quarterly* 19, no. 3 (2001): 51–59.

13. M. F. Robek, G. F. Brown, and D. O. Stephens, *Information and Records Management*, 4th ed. (New York: McGraw Hill, 1996) as quoted in Robert F. Nawrocki, "Electronic Records Management," *Encyclopedia of Library and Information Science* (New York: Marcel Dekker, 2003).

14. Johns Hopkins University Libraries, HERMES Project Web site, (Baltimore, Md.: Johns Hopkins University, 2004). Accessed 16 April 2005, http://hermes.mse.jhu.edu:8008/ hermesdocs/.

15. NISO and DLF, NISO/DLF Workshop on Standards for Electronic Resource Management, 10 May 2002. Accessed 16 April 2005, www.library.cornell.edu/cts/elicensestudy/nisodlf/home.htm. Materials, notes, and slides are posted.

16. Beth Forrest Warner, "Managing Electronic Resources in Today's ILMS Environment," (PowerPoint presentation from ALCTS E-resource Management Symposium, ALA Midwinter Meeting, Jan. 24, 2003). Accessed 16 April 2005, http://kudiglib.ku.edu/ Personal_prsns/ALA_Preconf_2003MW.htm; Beth Forrest Warner, "Managing Electronic Resources in Today's Integrated Library Management System Environment," *Electronic Resources Management* (Chicago: ALA, 2006).

17. Jewell, *Selection and Presentation*, 30.

18. CONSER: Cooperative Online Serials, Summit on Serials in the Digital Environment, March 18–19, 2004. Accessed 16 April 2005, www.loc.gov/acq/conser/summit.html.

19. Visionary Technology in Library Solutions, "VIEWS: A Newly Created Vendor Initiative for Enabling Web Services Announced," Press Release, 16 June 2004. Accessed 16 April 2005, www.vtls.com/Corporate/Releases/2004/21.shtml.

20. International Coalition of Library Consortia, "About the International Coalition of Library Consortia." Accessed 16 April 2005, www.library.yale.edu/consortia/.

21. COUNTER: Counting Online Usage of Networked Electronic Resources (Edinburgh, U.K.: COUNTER, 2004). Accessed 16 April 2005, www.projectcounter.org; Association of Research Libraries, "E-metrics: Measures for Electronic Resources" (Washington, D.C.: ARL, 2004). Accessed 16 April 2005, www.arl.org/stats/newmeas/ emetrics; University of Pennsylvania Libraries, "Penn Library Data Farm," (Philadelphia, Pa.: Univ. of Penn. Libraries, 2004). Accessed 16 April 2005, http://metrics .library.upenn.edu/prototype/about/index.html; Joseph Zucca, "Traces in the Clickstream: Early Work on a Management Information Repository at the University of Pennsylvania," *Information Technology and Libraries* 22, no. 4 (2003): 175–79.

Managing Electronic Resources in Today's Integrated Library Management System Environment

BETH FORREST WARNER

For at least a quarter of a century, libraries have tracked and provided access to selected electronic resources through integrated library management systems (ILMS). As collections move from print to electronic, the ILMS and internal library processes are challenged to efficiently provide comprehensive, integrated, accurate, timely, and user-accessible information about these resources. Today's environment and choices increase in complexity and the distinction blurs between the ILMS and evolving digital library systems and tools. Managers must identify a range of resource management issues for a variety of electronic resource types and make appropriate decisions about their use for their institutions.

The path to electronic access began with the printed card catalog and led through online catalogs, online databases, online journals, and the Web. During this transition, the introduction of a wide variety of electronic resources caused considerable confusion for librarians and library users alike. Librarians must now attempt to integrate resources such as e-journals, citation databases, and full-text article databases, as well as nonserial content such as e-books, government documents, numeric data sets, and spatial data, into a more coherent environment. Different types of content manipulation tools must also be integrated, because simply providing access to these resources without assistance for using them is unacceptable.

Distinctions between the resources the library owns and those to which it provides access are no longer clear. The library's resource profile must be modified to accommodate the variety of resource formats and the confusing range

This paper is based on a presentation made at the ALCTS Midwinter Symposium "Managing Electronic Resources: Meeting the Challenge," held in Philadelphia, January 2003.

of access methods. Different providers may offer the same content in different ways with varying degrees of completeness, so libraries must deal with issues of content versus carrier. As the volume of content increases, describing it accurately and efficiently becomes increasingly difficult. Libraries must address questions about rights management as they move from owning print content to accessing electronic content. What are libraries allowed to do with electronic materials? Who is allowed to access them? How long is that access available? All are critical questions that must be answered. Keeping track of content and aggregations is a challenge. Finally, there is the matter of trust. Libraries must trust the vendors they work with and, in turn, library users must trust the library to keep track of all the electronic resources and make them available in an accurate, timely, and usable fashion for the long term.

The Issues

The shifting environment has created a new set of resource management issues and challenges for the library community, which now must

- categorize what is owned, licensed, and collected;
- identify works of interest for specific communities of users from a wider range of possibilities;
- indicate where the identified resources are located—locally or remotely, individually or in an aggregation, institutionally or through cooperative agreements;
- explain the differences and nuances of what appear to be the same resources offered by several different services; and
- describe what can legally be done with the resources now and in the long term, once access has been established.

In short, doing what libraries have always done—bringing people and content together accurately, easily, and efficiently—seems to be getting more and more difficult in this new environment.

What is the typical user's response to these concerns? "Don't bother me with the details. Get me the stuff I want. Preferably online—and preferably right now!" Users' disinterest in the details compounds the problems and challenges for libraries to provide them with the correct content in a coherent, usable environment without all the messiness that surrounds electronic resources. Some key management issues include:

- identifying resources;
- acquiring ownership of and access to those resources;

- tracking ownership and access;
- describing materials;
- integrating the resources, including searching and presentation issues;
- developing user support and instruction; and
- evaluating resources on a continuing basis.

Upon close inspection, these management issues are reasonably well-aligned with the following functions of the basic ILMS:

- acquisitions and serials control—identifying and acquiring resources and tracking ownership;
- cataloging and holdings management—providing bibliographic control and description, including authorities;
- circulation—controlling access;
- online public access catalog (OPAC)—providing public access; and
- reporting and statistics—evaluating resources and their use.

Although a case may be made that there is a correlation between ILMS functions and electronic resource management (ERM) issues, the question actually is whether the ILMS can *sufficiently* meet the complex management needs of the online resource environment. In order to answer this question, the basic ILMS functions should be reexamined to determine if they are appropriate to manage electronic resources.

Functionality

Libraries traditionally acquired material that was locally owned and physically maintained in the library. Libraries now deal with resources that are more than simply owned. A tracking mechanism has become necessary, particularly when information about a resource is assembled well before the decision to acquire is made. Tracking has become an incredibly complex task. More and more details about material must be managed and local and consortial decisions must be accommodated. Who has access to the material and under what conditions? Who manages the aggregations, the variety of titles, and the overlap that exists? Who takes care of things when the content of a resource changes—sometimes overnight and without warning? Essential information about payments and fund management must be maintained, as must details of consortial agreements and bundled deals. In addition, technical management information—the IP ranges, whom to call for hardware and software support and proxy management—must be stored and be accessible at a moment's notice.

Bibliographic tools such as machine-readable cataloging (MARC), Library of Congress Subject Headings (LCSH), and Dewey are well-suited to manage the resources found in the print environment. In the electronic environment, the volatile nature of many resources makes managing the materials much more complex. A variety of new metadata formats and specialized thesauri have been devised to deal with this shifting environment. Linking these new tools to each other and to traditional descriptive tools is critical.

To address the needs of this evolving environment, the MARC format must be reevaluated and, if possible, made more nimble so that it can handle the variety and mutability of available resources. In the meantime, emerging metadata formats must be integrated with what has traditionally been the MARC-based environment of the ILMS. Libraries need to improve ways of dealing with multiple manifestations of the same content—print, electronic, different versions of the electronic, and the variety of formats including print, extensible-markup language (XML), portable document format (PDF), and standard generalized markup language (SGML). Authority control in a fluid, uncontrolled environment is almost an exercise in futility, yet that added value is still important. Finding efficient ways to manage these volatile resources with minimal staff support is the key.

Libraries ultimately must decide how much detail users need to conduct successful online searches. Given the growing body of full-text content available online and accessible by increasingly powerful search tools, libraries must be more deliberate in determining the level of description applied to various types of resources, as opposed to the self-description of full-content access, in order to provide adequate resource discovery.

Once resources have been described, they must be located. In the traditional library setting, owned items are organized by call number: the number is assigned, the item goes on the shelf, and the number remains unchanged for an indefinite period, which creates a relatively stable retrieval environment. In this new environment, libraries must deal not only with physical objects but also provide direct links to external electronic objects. Now, in addition to dealing with orderly, numbered items, librarians must account for licensed or freely accessible items with volatile uniform resource locators (URLs). Dealing with URLs can be a major challenge, especially if there are thousands of them in the cataloging records and a system manager decides to reorganize storage directories—a very unstable environment. Suddenly, all the URLs are incorrect and identifying and correcting all the records can be a very time-consuming task. Given the current volatility of URLs, mechanisms must be incorporated to easily and accurately maintain and stabilize them for the long term.

Libraries must find effective ways to accurately track holdings over time. This includes bringing multiple manifestations of an item together and dealing with appropriate copy issues so that the colocated versions of an item are not only correct but that access rights and mechanisms are clearly delineated for the user. Library staff need to track holdings from aggregators on a day-to-day basis and verify that they have access to the resources to which they are entitled. In this largely uncontrolled environment, tracking and monitoring the many available resources is an urgent necessity and is (together with URL management) one of the more difficult tasks facing librarians.

Access control has routinely been equated to circulation of physical pieces. Now libraries find they must also control virtual access by using such processes as IP-range management and authentication and authorization. In addition, libraries serve on-campus and now remote users. Serving this new user group raises an entirely new set of concerns. Licensing provisions must be carefully studied and interpreted—all licenses are not created equal—and libraries must integrate their activities much more closely with those of their parent institutions so that identification, authentication, and authorization can be satisfactorily managed. The library must know not only who their users are but also where they are—on-site or off-site—and make sure users can access the resources regardless of location.

The OPAC brings the support functions of the ILMS together for public consumption. Locally held materials were accessed through the OPAC; searching, abstracting, and indexing services have been controlled by MARC and LCSH structures. However, in today's environment, libraries deal with access to local *and* remote materials, search against controlled *and* uncontrolled records, and handle multiple resources *and* multiple sources. Bringing all these aspects together in a way that is intelligible to users has become much more complicated. Libraries must present and interpret the provisions of a licensing agreement to users so what can and cannot be done with accessible materials is clear. The library's infrastructure can no longer be maintained separately, but must be integrated with other institutional infrastructures to establish and maintain adequate mechanisms to identify, authorize, and authenticate users, including distance learners and remote users. Amalgamating multiple resources that libraries acquire and combining multiple record formats, records, and search types into one, easily usable structure must be accomplished. Is it possible to bring these elements together in a way that does not confuse users—and, is the ILMS the appropriate vehicle to accomplish this?

Having provided these resources, are they used, and if so, by whom? Are they useful? Unfortunately, questions like these are often an afterthought and answers, when offered, are usually basic, simplistic, and do not provide a great deal of helpful information. In the traditional library setting, circulation statistics—the number of loans, interlibrary loans, and the number of database searches—provide some answers. In the electronic setting, detailed, sophisticated reports and statistics need to be developed and should include such information as which resources have been accessed, how much Web use there is, and what sort of cost-benefit analysis can be obtained. Building a coherent picture of what users are doing and what is being used depends on libraries defining the measures that are relevant in today's environment. In the past, such organizations as the Association of Research Libraries (ARL) have rewarded libraries for the quantity of material that was collected, but not necessarily for how or even whether that material was used. While such initiatives as Counting Online Usage of Networked Electronic Resources (COUNTER) and the E-Metrics project begin to change practices, measures must be developed to more accurately reflect the relevance of the information that libraries provide to their users. Just as there are many ways to gain access to information, there are many ways to count and measure that access. Libraries need to determine which measures are critical and will give them the information they need in order to make informed decisions and to determine the relevance of the resources provided.

The Options

In order to translate these management requirements into functionality, the following issues need to be considered:

> Providing better mechanisms for evaluating resources prior to acquisition and better ways to easily share and update information, as well as better methods of tracking the process and sharing status information.

> Interpreting, categorizing, tracking, and publicizing license provisions.

> Managing resources that are freely available, tracking them, keeping them up to date, and incorporating them within the framework of other resources.

> Accommodating new metadata formats designed by different communities of interest, such as Dublin Core, Virtual Resources Association (VRA), encoded archival description (EAD), Federal Geographic Data Community (FGDC), and providing bibliographic translations between formats.

> Tracking the various components and multiple manifestations of a resource supplied by multiple providers and providing users with accurate information on its availability.

> Organizing content and links when resources are volatile and their half-life on the Web is fleeting at best.

Providing better resource discovery functions by introducing a variety of traditional and emerging methods, such as federated or metasearching to execute searches across multiple, remote, independent resources. While Z39.50 connections to multiple library catalogs and other selected resources is a start, this concept must be expanded into a disparate resource environment that does not consist solely of Z39.50-compliant systems. Another option is aggregating information harvested from a variety of sources into a centralized service where the search is performed. In addition to streamlining the process, providing better nontextual resource discovery methods with tools like visualization techniques, clustering, image recognition, and audio pattern recognition is vital. Each approach has its pros and cons, so it is important to determine the best choice based on a particular environment, a set of resources, and a specific group of users. A combination of approaches may be what is ultimately needed.

Institutional identity is an extremely important component in providing a successful electronic environment. Resource-independent institutional infrastructures and systems should be used whenever possible to give users more accurate and convenient access control. Libraries should not have to manage multiple passwords nor should users be required to remember multiple passwords. Single sign-on is today's mantra.

Measuring the success (or lack) of delivering resources must be systematized. Does a hit actually mean that the user was successful in finding the information he or she wanted?

Finally, accurate access to resources and system troubleshooting information must be readily available online to users at all times.

How well does today's ILMS meet these needs? The key to answering this question may be found in how one defines the basic ILMS. The *I* in ILMS stands for integrated. It can perhaps be extended to stand for interoperable. However, it cannot be stretched to stand for all-inclusive. The *I* in ILMS must be redefined and refocused. It is time to focus on integrating the library management system as the core of a group of extended functions rather than attempting to create a monolithic, comprehensive system. It is time to define integrated not as integrated within the ILMS, but as the ILMS integrated into a broader functional environment. It is time to move from the model in which the ILMS tries to do everything to a model in which the ILMS is one of several components used to provide total management control; into what might be better referred to as a resource management environment (RME).

The Future

Openness, interoperability, and integration with external systems and services are key characteristics of this new environment. Standard data formats and standardized application interfaces should be reviewed carefully, with an emphasis on XML. Standard data transfer protocols should be used for moving information across systems. Looking beyond current library standards and begining to take better advantage of relevant, external industry standards is imperative. Other characteristics of the emerging RME include the following.

ERM

The Digital Library Federation (DLF) issued a report that defines ERM and details the components of ERM functionality.[1] At the same time, ILMS vendors are developing new modules to be integrated with existing ILMS systems or to be used as stand-alone systems. These developments depend on common, open standards that easily and accurately move data into and out of these modules. These systems will be successful and attractive to users if data are accessible and transparent and the systems utilize open formats and interfaces that anyone can link to (rather than proprietary formats).

Metadata and Extended Description Initiatives

Integrating the increasing variety of metadata formats is a daunting task. Should they be shoehorned into the MARC-based catalog, or are there ways to bring these diverse formats together dynamically in intelligible, integrated information displays? Much will depend on creating accurate crosswalks, looking closely at record-content definitions, including extended resource descriptions, and finding creative data integration solutions. An overview of this issue and some potential approaches can be found through OCLC's Research Office.[2]

Content Management Services

Services for such remote resources as e-journal management systems, e-book delivery systems, or such dataset registration/repository services as those provided by the Interuniversity Consortium for Political and Social Research (ICPSR) need to be reviewed, and decisions need to be made regarding effectively using the information they provide and integrating it into existing systems for precise resources management.[3]

Linking Standards

Effective access and resource management depend on linking standards. How is information linked across different resources? An entire industry is being developed around the OpenURL standard, which matches content components across disparate resources. OpenURL is a generic Web technology that enables the context of a service request to be evaluated within the user environment (i.e., the user's institution is allowed to determine the link endpoints). For example, OpenURL can transparently link a user to a citation in one resource to the actual object in a separate resource.

Search Protocols

Libraries need to look at how different search protocols are integrated. Tools for integrating protocols such as Z39.50, HTTP, and XML gateways, are being developed. Libraries must decide whether their users should be aware of these protocols, or if it is better to develop systems that take advantage of the strengths of each protocol, keeping them behind the scenes. This emerging environment should include new discovery methods, such as federation and aggregation, and Web services, which enable content delivery through standardized Web protocols.

Authorization and Authentication Services

One major component in resource and access management involves moving away from IP-range authentication toward credentialing services and middleware components for controlling access. For example, middleware (being developed through the Internet2 Shibboleth project) with credentialing (directory) services (e.g., PKI or EduPerson) will help libraries manage services more easily and make the services more secure and more readily available to users.[4] Eliminating individual passwords for a variety of different resources will make it easier to manage proxy services and more efficient to share materials consortially. Introduction of middleware services such as those noted above will make the resource environment more consistent for all users, whether they are on campus or at a remote location.

Resource Management Statistics

Measuring service is a key component of the new resource environment. Such initiatives as ARL's LibQual+ and E-Metrics are considering how library services and access to resources are measured in this new environment. It is no longer enough to evaluate services by counting the number of physical pieces held in the library.[5] The emphasis must be shifted from the number of volumes held or added to the collection to other units of measurement that actually determine how the material is used. What tools can be used to determine successful access and how are these new measurements best explained to faculty and administrators?

Conclusion

The redefined ILMS can be a core component of the new electronic resource management environment. Understanding the nature of the ILMS and making sure that it continues to do well the things it was designed to do are essential if this is to happen. Once this is accomplished, the openness and interoperability of today's systems need to be enhanced to more easily and accurately communicate with external systems. Existing industry standards for new services must be invoked. Time should be spent developing solutions to problems that are truly unique to the library environment, rather than spending time reinventing solutions available in the broader information industry. This applies particularly to the area of standards development, where a great deal of time is being spent developing new standards when existing industry standards would be quite adequate. The advantage to making the ILMS a core component of a broader ERM environment is that external systems can be accommodated more easily in the long run, particularly as new environments are explored and introduced.

Is the ILMS well-positioned to address the current and future resource management needs of the library? The answer depends, ultimately, on the expectations libraries have for this individual system. The ILMS can no longer provide a solution for all of the library's resource management needs and should become a component in a much broader system. Today's information resources are too complex to be managed by a one-size-fits-all solution. The ILMS cannot be all things to all people and shouldn't try to be. Rather, the system should focus on doing what it has always done best: providing basic functionality for core library operations. Open, standards-based, interoperable systems that exploit the truly unique aspects of the bibliographic and resource control environment should be developed and implemented. At the same time, librarians need to take advantage of new, external, non-ILMS systems in which to more effectively and quickly integrate and improve their ability to manage the resource and service environments libraries face today.

REFERENCE NOTES

1. Timothy D. Jewell et al., *Electronic Resource Management: The Report of the DLF ERM Initiative* (Washington, D.C.: Digital Library Federation, 2004). Accessed 16 April 2005, www.diglib.org/pubs/dlfermi0408/.

2. For example, OCLC, "Metadata Switch" (Dublin, Ohio: OCLC, 2005). Accessed 16 April 2005, www.oclc.org/research/projects/mswitch; Carol Jean Godby, Devon Smith, and Eric Childress, "Two Paths to Interoperable Metadata," Paper presented at the 2003 Dublin Core Conference, DC–2003: Supporting Communities of Discourse and Practice—Metadata Research & Applications, September 28–October 2, Seattle, Washington. Accessed 16 April 2005, www.oclc.org/research/publications/archive/2003/godby-dc2003.pdf.

3. Interuniversity Consortium for Political and Social Research (Ann Arbor, Mich.: Institute for Social Research of the University of Michigan, 2005). Accessed 16 April 2005, www.icpsr.org. This organization maintains and provides access to a vast archive of social science data for research and instruction.

4. Internet2, Shibboleth Project Web page (Ann Arbor, Mich.: Internet2, 2005). Accessed 16 April 2005, http://shibboleth.internet2.edu; Internet2, EDUCAUSE, and Net@EDU, "Higher Education Public Key Infrastructure Technical Activities Group" (Ann Arbor, Mich.: Internet2, 2005). Accessed 16 April 2005, http://middleware.internet2.edu/hepki-tag; EDUCAUSE/ Internet2, "eduPerson Object Class" (Boulder, Colo.: EDUCAUSE, 2005). Accessed 16 April 2005, www.educause.edu/eduperson.

5. Association of Research Libraries, "LibQUAL+ Web site" (Washington, D.C.: ARL, 2005). Accessed 16 April 2005, www.libqual.org/; Association of Research Libraries, "E-Metrics: Measures for Electronic Resources" (Washington, D.C.: ARL, 2005). Accessed 16 April 2005, www.arl.org/stats/newmeas/emetrics/index.html.

The Three A's of E-resource Management

Aggravation, Agitation, and Aggregation

DAN TONKERY

In the print environment, subscription agents successfully reduced library workloads, and one can argue that there is an even greater role for subscription agents in e-journal management. While some publishers have attempted to bypass subscription agents and work directly with libraries, there is a growing sense within the library community that the work involved in acquiring electronic resources directly from publishers is excessive and that few libraries have the staff for the extra tasks of direct ordering. Simple tasks like producing an invoice or issuing a credit can be burdensome for some publishers. As long as a high level of detail work is required to manage subscriptions for electronic resources, agents will have an important role to play in supporting libraries through the print-to-electronic transition and well into the digital library era.

Background

Six important issues must be outlined before the roots of the aggravation involved in managing electronic resources are explored.

1. *Electronic resources have a major impact on libraries, publishers, and subscription agents.*

   For thousands of journals, the shift from print to electronic formats has had a major cost impact on communities involved in creation, distribution,

This paper is based on a presentation made at the ALCTS Midwinter Symposium "Managing Electronic Resources: Meeting the Challenge," held in Philadelphia, January 2003. It has been updated to reflect recent changes in the library marketplace.

access, and customer support functions. Every publisher involved in e-journal distribution has had to make an enormous investment in creating a new workflow or revising an old one. In fact, many publishers have created a separate unit to handle electronic products. Subscription agents have reengineered their processing systems to control ordering, renewing, and managing electronic subscriptions. Libraries have had to learn to deal with licenses and registrations. The bottom line is that the workflow that presently supports e-resources is too costly for every segment in the information chain. Everyone involved is making serious investments to change processes and create and implement better management tools. Moreover, each sector deals with both print and electronic formats and maintaining workflows for both is expensive. Finally, libraries—which had hoped to see a savings with electronic distribution of scholarly journals—have been frustrated as the anticipated cost savings from the shift in formats has not occurred.

2. *End users want content delivered to their desktops and they often do not understand that the information in question is not free.*

Every usage study that has been conducted has produced similar results. In general, students and faculty enthusiastically support the desktop delivery of information and would prefer that all materials be presented in that format. In fact, users want more depth of coverage—not only the last five years in electronic format but entire runs of journals back to volume one, number one. Some libraries are shifting their acquisitions strategy and dropping print in order to acquire materials only in electronic form. Publishers have recognized this trend and, in response, have begun to develop new pricing models that protect their subscription revenue base while allowing libraries the flexibility to collect in a preferred format. Access to the electronic format is no longer tied to the print subscription. However, librarians need to educate their users and the administrations of their institutions about the costs associated with all this content.

3. *For ten years, libraries reduced the size of their technical services staff.*

With improvements in productivity as a result of implementing integrated library systems (ILS) and from participation in bibliographic utilities, many positions in acquisitions, cataloging, and serials departments, among both the professional and support staff ranks, have been reduced or shifted elsewhere in the library to support new services. Consequently, libraries now lack the personnel resources required to support extensive manual processing of print materials and adequately handle the labor-intensive workflows needed to support e-resources access and management.

4. *The workflow required to support e-resources is complex, complicated, and costly.*

   Libraries with growing collections of electronic journals and other electronic resources are finding that the amount of work required to provide access to and management of these materials can be five to ten times as much work as supporting print subscriptions. Libraries have also learned that, until recently, there were few automated solutions available for support. Because neither ILS nor subscription agents had a set of tools to support the new workflow, many large research libraries—and some smaller libraries as well—have started to build their own electronic resource management (ERM) systems.

5. *Publishers are still experimenting with delivery systems, acquisitions models, and pricing strategies.*

   The shift from print to electronic formats has had a major impact on publishers, who have been investing in new delivery systems and often been coping with dual workflows. Almost every publisher began distributing e-versions of their publications at no additional cost when linked to existing print subscriptions, but this free-with-print model has been short lived. Many publishers have now adopted one of a variety of pricing models, including e-content–only pricing. They continue to experiment with different models and make modifications as they gain insight into the changing market conditions. Not only have publishers changed pricing models, but they are also moving to different hosting services. In addition, they continue to protect their intellectual property rights with license agreements that include terms and conditions that are often hard for a library to interpret or enforce.

6. *The cost of set-up, renewal, and maintenance of e-resources is a burden to all the players in this industry.*

   Everyone in this industry—publishers, subscription agencies, and libraries— is having difficulty managing the workflow required by e-resources. Subscription agents have been working to re-engineer their processing systems to support additional new management services. Publishers have set up new or expanded customer services groups. Libraries have created new positions, such as electronic resources managers, and have had to shift staff from other departments and services to manage the access and management functions. Everyone agrees that the amount of work required to maintain an active e-resource subscription is greater than should be necessary. However, the industry lacks tools to streamline the workload.

Aggravation

In many libraries, managing electronic resources is a complex and time-consuming process. It has been made even more difficult by the explosive growth of journals and other resources that are available online, by the sheer complexity of obtaining access, and by the intellectual property conditions that have been established by publishers attempting to determine the best system of pricing and controls to protect their intellectual property. Many librarians working in the electronic resource environment have a high level of frustration and a growing feeling of aggravation with what they believe should be the most exciting new opportunity to arrive on their doorstep since the invention of movable type.

While end users' appetites for electronic information are almost insatiable, libraries that have to support the shift from print to digital resources are drowning in seas of make-work that are not alleviated by information suppliers. The acquisitions functions of electronic resources are at best only partially supported in the various ILS. Most acquisitions modules have not been designed to incorporate the necessary metadata related to electronic resources, nor have the ILS been designed to provide adequate control or management of electronic resources.

Intensifying the aggravation is the shift from ownership to leasing. Libraries no longer own the content, instead they lease it under the terms of a license that restricts usage according to a set of terms and conditions. As a result, librarians have established control systems that limit or restrict access according to who and where users are in order to satisfy publishers who have established a complex set of user definitions that must be enforced by the library in order to avoid losing access altogether. At the very least, violations of a license agreement can result in a service interruption. For example, many libraries have found out that publishers monitor usage at a gross level and turn off access when license terms are violated.

Licensing is only the first step in providing successful access to end users. It is often a long and complex process that involves several individuals in an organization. Tracking a license as it wends its way through the system is complex and often lacks adequate control. Many libraries have had to develop local tracking systems to manage the process. In large libraries where several hundred licenses, each with a different set of terms and conditions, must be tracked, aggravation runs high. The terms and conditions vary greatly from library to library, and it is not uncommon for a library to negotiate special rates based on controlled access to materials. As a result, libraries may need to implement a variety of access control methods. The tracking systems they develop must have the capability to identify these variations both internally to staff as well as externally to users.

The steps involved in registration and access can be difficult to determine and frequently change as publishers experiment with different hosting services. Because current ILS do not adequately support the metadata needed to control registration functions, librarians are faced with finding a solution that will enable them to control and manage an ever-increasing, sometimes substantial part of their collections. Several of the largest research libraries—including Penn State, MIT, Johns Hopkins, and UCLA—have developed local solutions. However, building stand-alone systems is not a long-term solution, and even these institutions with outstanding model systems recognize the need for commercial systems to be built and maintained. Librarians are looking for flexible systems that will integrate with the processing systems they already have in place.

A number of libraries have been working on a cooperative project sponsored by the Digital Library Federation (DLF). The DLF Electronic Resource Management Initiative (ERMI), under the direction of Timothy D. Jewell (University of Washington), built a set of specifications that identifies the metadata needed to control electronic resources in an ILS. The initiative was optimistic that a group of large research libraries, pooling their collective knowledge and resources, could be instrumental in developing the specifications for e-resource management modules.[1]

Aggravation Often Leads to Agitation

While the lack of suitable systems aggravates librarians, agitation stems from the way that electronic resources tend to be packaged and sold. Publisher pricing and access models have become a sore spot for many librarians faced with difficult budget situations. The biggest issue to date has revolved around the concept of the Big Deal, wherein a library, a library system, or even a consortium is required by contract to maintain a set level of expenditures during a fixed period of time, often three to five years. Libraries that agree to these types of arrangements commit a major portion of their materials budget in advance. While this may provide them with online access to a large number of quality journals, they also may end up with titles they would not normally choose to acquire and without the resources to continue ongoing subscriptions or to place new subscriptions with other publishers. In effect, the library's collection development strategy is artificially controlled by the Big Deal, which eventually may be viewed more as a drawback than as an asset, as it locks up too much of the budget. Some libraries have decided to forego these types of multiyear contracts, while others are still scrambling to find funds to continue to provide access to the wide array of resources.

Other situations that create agitation include having to maintain print subscriptions in order to obtain access to electronic versions, or having to maintain print subscriptions in case a publisher pulls the plug on all online access, leaving the library with nothing to show for its payments. Libraries need to have flexible licensing and acquisitions arrangements that allow them to respond to changing economic conditions and control their collection development strategy. For example, libraries need to know that licenses agreed to and money spent on resources now will ensure access for future generations of users. Some faculty and researchers understand that Big Deals and print archives have an unrealistic cost, while others still need to be educated.

So What Does the Subscription Agent Offer? Data Aggregation, for One Thing!

How can subscription agencies alleviate the librarians' aggravation and agitation? By providing data aggregation! Subscription agents have a long history of offering value-added services that have served libraries well in the print environment. Subscribtion agents have developed online systems to allow them to communicate with their library customers, and they have offered productivity tools, such as invoice loads and online claiming support that enable libraries to transfer data to their local ILS. Agents have built a variety of collection development reports that identify pricing trends and other related functions.

As information shifts from a print to a digital environment, the trusted agency of the past that offered a variety of subscription management tools is beginning to offer a new set of tools to help customers cope with access and management of electronic resources. Agents are good at data collection, record management, handling payments, and recording financial transactions. They maintain close relationships with publishers, and in addition to tracking titles are now learning to track license terms and conditions, a variety of pricing options, and metadata about titles. Agents maintain publisher addresses and contact points for customer service and technical support. In short, much of what agents have done for print subscriptions is being carried over and enhanced to support e-journal access and management requirements in this expanded digital environment.

Examining the life cycle of an electronic resource may be useful in understanding how subscription agents can assist librarians in managing their electronic resources. Figure 1 illustrates how complex electronic resources are to acquire, access, and manage in comparison to print resources. Even though serials management has been traditionally viewed as one of the most complicated library functions, managing electronic resources elevates the workload and management skills to new levels.

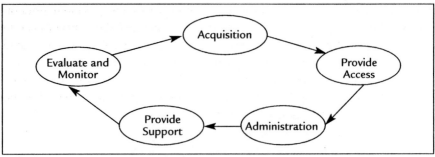

FIGURE 1 | E-resources Life Cycle

Acquisition

The life cycle of an electronic resource has five major components and sub-scription agencies have a role in each. First is the acquisitions phase, the stage of the agent's traditional strength. Subscription agencies have established substantial knowledge bases consisting of information or metadata about publishers in general and about the specific titles they publish. Provided that a publisher will let a subscription agency handle library orders, the agent is able to process and manage the order whether the library is acquiring the title or whether the title is acquired on the basis of a special or consortial arrangement. The agent processes orders and handles renewals and captures the metadata required to activate the order, including sending the publisher's hosting service the library's IP address ranges. The agent's system can handle all the processing tasks associated with an order. Almost all publishers require libraries to enter into some form of license agreement to control intellectual property. Subscription agencies can assist libraries with license negotiations if necessary.

Provide Access

Once the details of acquisition have been resolved, the library must decide which access method is appropriate for its needs. Many libraries will use a subscription agent's access system. Others use a combination of agent systems and publisher systems. Both are supported by the agent, as subscription agencies actively capture and maintain uniform resource locators (URLs).

Regardless of the method of access, proper registration with the publisher is mandatory. Registration is a library function and one not fully supported by any other member of the information chain. The registration phase can be complex and difficult to manage, particularly when a collection of electronic resources is large and obtained through diverse channels. Subscription agencies can support registration in cases where publishers will allow them to register on behalf of libraries. However, when publishers operate closed systems or need to echo (ping) a library's IP address range, subscription agencies may not be able to assist in registration. Agents have been creative, working with a number of the hosting services to establish streamlined workflows that allow them to update access systems. The goal should be to receive an order and establish service the same day, or within twenty-four hours of receipt of the order.

Administration

Even after titles are registered and access is enabled, problems with access can occur. Subscription agencies maintain extensive knowledge databases with contact information so that when problems happen, regardless of the nature of the problem, the agent can provide the library with a contact, or can serve as the middleman between the library and the publisher in order to quickly correct the problem. For libraries, gathering and maintaining full contact information can be a major undertaking whereas subscription agencies gather such information routinely. There are also economies of scale—the information in the agent's files can help hundreds of customers. In addition, agencies can often help diagnose problems and provide e-mail addresses, telephone numbers, or hotline information required to solve service issues.

Subscription agencies' greatest assets are the knowledge bases they develop and continually maintain with information provided by the organizations that produce content. With more than 16,000 different publishers publishing more than 400,000 print titles, agencies have a solid information base upon which to build. Agencies now routinely gather registration information for more than 16,000 electronic titles from more than 1,200 publishers.

The knowledge bases maintained by subscription agents have been expanded to include the names of the people who handle the orders. Many publishers have a separate workflow for electronic orders, so agencies routinely collect and track two sets of contact names—those who handle print and those who handle online resources. Subscription agencies are also building an inventory of registration instructions that include details on how and where to register as well as information on pinging and where IP addresses can be maintained when changes are necessary.

Provide Support

Subscription agents routinely handle URL maintenance, sort out registration issues, and expedite payment to publishers through credit card or wire transfer so that librarians can provide end users with access to e-resources as quickly as possible. Subscription agents are trusted and often able to resolve problems for hundreds of clients with a single action.

Evaluate and Monitor

To assist in the evaluation of the e-journal collection, the library can use the agent's e-journal access system to capture the user traffic that goes through the agent's service. Usage data collected in one place is more effective than trying to manage the data collected from many hosts. While the industry is making strides to standardize the data through such initiatives as Counting Online Usage of NeTworked Electronic Resources, the agent can be relied upon to collect usage data through its systems so that the library has data to review before negotiating renewal contracts.

Conclusion

Subscription agents have the potential to offer an even wider range of support tasks. They have already been involved in license negotiation on behalf of some libraries and could readily use their experience and their extensive knowledge base of licensing procedures to support workflow in their customers' libraries. Subscription agents are in an excellent position to automate or support many of the licensing and registration tasks related to ERM. Agents may be able to provide workflow management software that can be used by an individual library to manage the license process if a library wishes to retain control of the negotiation process.

In the future, registration tasks are likely to become increasingly automated as a number of software applications provide relief in this labor-intensive area of ERM. For now, however, a subscription agent can supply a knowledge base of registration procedures and offer a place for customer registration data to be recorded.

The key to effective ERM is building a knowledge base of licensing and registration procedures for the array of publishers, aggregators, and hosting services involved in e-resource provision. Someone must build a system that allows libraries to capture and maintain their unique licensing and registration data in a database that supports workflow management, problem tracking, and registration support. Eventually, ILS vendors, subscription agencies, or some other organization will fill this void by providing the management tools librarians need.

Subscription agencies are in a unique position to create such knowledge bases because they already maintain a broad range of details about the electronic resources that are available, along with extensive metadata about the resources, a comprehensive file of licensing and registration procedures, as well as contact data for all types of technical support. Agents have always been good at collecting data and managing the "many-to-one" relationship. It is not cost-effective for hundreds or even thousands of libraries to collect the same data when subscription agencies already collect that data and can easily share it with all of their customers. Of course, these services could not be offered to libraries free of charge, but would have to be priced separately or built into service charges.

In the e-resource environment, the value-added services for which subscription agencies have become known will continue to be enhanced. Agents have proven to be successful middlemen; they have the core skill set, the expertise, the publisher relationships, and the systems knowledge to collect and build an effective knowledge base to support e-resources.

Agents are already supporting a new range of services such as link revolvers and access services. In the not too distant future, they will begin to offer a number of new services in the areas of licensing, registration, and access to e-resources. Subscription agencies have the capability to deliver the full range of services that librarians need to manage the explosion in electronic resources now and well into the future.

REFERENCE NOTE

1. Digital Library Federation, "Electronic Resource Management Initiative" (Washington, D.C.: DLF, 2004). Accessed 16 April 2005, www.diglib.org/standards/dlf-erm02.htm.

House of Horrors

Exorcising Electronic Resources

NORM MEDEIROS

Electronic resources, especially electronic journals, are maddening. Come to think of it, print serials have never been much fun to deal with either. C. Sumner Spalding, writing in 1957 and in a tone appropriate for the science fiction craze of the time, summarized well the frustrations serials catalogers experience:

> Whereas monographs are normally received in their fully-developed form, physically static, ossified, and dead, so to speak, serials are generally received alive, growing, and subject to various unpredictable metamorphoses. The problem of describing something which is alive and which may at any time in the future assume relationships with others of its kind . . . is of a different order from that of describing something which can be counted on to lie still and not move while we take its measure and describe it[s] characteristics once and for all.[1]

Thirty years after Spalding's remarks, Syracuse University's *New Horizons in Adult Education* electronic journal debuted, the first of a prolific species that often make librarians feel nostalgic about their Kardex days.

To better understand today's crazy world of electronic resources, librarians need to reflect on the evolution of the e-journal. Like Spalding, another editor of the *Anglo-American Cataloging Rules*, Michael Gorman, published an article in 1991 in which he made certain predictions about libraries in the coming decade. Not surprisingly, many of his predictions came true. One remarkably incorrect predication, however, was that the impact of electronic journals

---

This paper is based on a presentation made at the ALCTS Midwinter Symposium "Taming the Electronic Tiger: Effective Management of E-resources," held in San Diego, January 2004.

would "rise from the invisible to the miniscule in the next five years," and will be "unimportant" in 2001.[2] One really cannot blame Gorman for miscalculating the impact electronic publishing would have on libraries. When he wrote this article, there were only eight peer-reviewed electronic journals in existence, produced by pioneering academics at such institutions as Virginia Tech, Princeton, and the aforementioned Syracuse University. Electronic journals from commercial publishers were nowhere to be seen. Today, 75 percent of the scholarly journals published offer online access, with few, if any, commercial publishers not in the game.[3]

These early e-journals were sent to subscribers as issues appeared. Occasionally, a subscriber would receive notification that an issue was ready, and a command would be sent to receive the full text. As early as 1990, libraries began worrying about archival access to these publications and many began to store copies of e-journals either electronically or in print.[4] Because the publishers of these early e-journals were academics, there were no guarantees regarding the duration of publication. If an editor decided to stop issuing the e-journal or moved to another institution, there was no telling what might happen to the scholarship he or she had overseen. Naturally, there was great concern over the transient nature of this new publishing process, not to mention questions about how libraries would make these journals available to their patrons. In these pre-Web days, library staff used dumb terminals to access OCLC and mainframe-based library systems. BITNET and fledgling Internet e-mail were recent innovations, and text-based Gopher servers made their first appearances. There were no standards for cataloging electronic journals, and certainly no best practice guidelines to help libraries provide access to these resources.

Despite these problems, in hindsight, there was much good fortune. By 1995, there were almost one hundred peer-reviewed e-journals in existence.[5] Serialists in the early 1990s also benefited from knowing what had been published. Subscribers were notified of new issues and action could then be taken to process these issues. At Virginia Tech, for example, processing electronic journals followed the same procedures as processing print serials.[6] Issues were checked in and claimed as necessary. It is hard to imagine doing this today given the hundreds or thousands of e-journals to which many academic libraries provide access. Furthermore, demand for these early e-journals was low, so libraries were able to experiment with procedures and workflows. It was truly a grace period that ended when the Mosaic browser illuminated the Web.

Web Revolution

Mosaic was released in 1993. It was the first widely used graphical browser and within eighteen months of its release helped bring about the Web revolution.

On the heels of this innovation was the implementation of OCLC's Internet Cataloging Project in 1994. The following year, the MARC 856 field was approved, turning the online public access catalog (OPAC) from atlas to vehicle of information delivery and spawning rapid development of Web-enabled catalogs by OPAC vendors. Also in 1995, the first edition of Nancy B. Olson's seminal guide to cataloging Internet resources was published.[7] Amidst the innumerable changes resulting from Mosaic and the Web, publishers began tinkering with online access to their journals. Looking back, it seems ridiculous, but at the time no one knew if print journals delivered through the Web would be popular or marketable. In part because of this uncertainty, many publishers simply gave institutions access to their online content on the basis of print subscriptions. Libraries spent hours determining how to catalog these resources. Fledgling Web site developers put up annotated e-journal lists, and not remarkably, people used them. Some technically competent professors—at that time defined as those who regularly used e-mail—took advantage of the new offerings. Libraries didn't mind providing the service as the resources were free, and although catalogers and Web personnel were required to create bibliographic records and Web lists, the effort seemed worthwhile. In fact, in the mid-1990s, many academic libraries led the way in creating a Web presence on campus. Development of e-journal lists was among the first value-added content to grace these pages.

Almost overnight, providing access to electronic journals was seen as one of the most important aspects of technical services. Jim Holmes, head of serials cataloging at the University of Texas (UT) at Austin, accurately described the impact when he wrote:

> Some time late in 1995, an e-mail message arrived in technical services from the Associate Director for Technical Services. She was so excited about [uniform resource locators] URLs and told technical services that it should also be excited and should be giving URLs a lot of thought. About 100 fingers pressed the delete button, trashed the message, and got back to cataloging the *Newsletter of the Texas Republic.*[8]

Despite that initial reaction, Jim reported that, within months UT Austin had purchased access to the collections of the Scholarly Journal Archive (JSTOR), Project Muse, and the American Institute of Physics, representing more than 6,000 URLs. The old adage about job security was not comforting.

Access versus Ownership

During this period, ideological debates about the role of the catalog raged. Should it be an inventory list or a finding aid? Regina Reynolds, head of the National Serials Data Program at the Library of Congress, wrote an especially compelling piece about this issue.[9] While she questioned the value of pointing to remote files through the catalog, suggesting that the practice could mislead users, she also admitted that the transformation of the catalog from inventory list to information gateway was inevitable. Despite this debate, many libraries began adding records for e-resources to their catalogs and exploiting Web-enabled OPACs, and by the mid-1990s redundant access to e-journals, both through the catalog as well as through hand-coded Web pages, was fairly common. The appearance of bibliographic records for e-resources in OCLC during this period was welcomed by the cataloging community, but these records often needed significant editing to account for mode of access and other differences between the library that provided the original bibliographic record and the library adapting the record for local use. In 1996, Cooperative Online Serials (CONSER) approved a single-record approach for cataloging e-journals also held in print. At first, this seemed to alleviate some of the cataloging work, but later this practice proved to be problematic for libraries that received the same e-journal from two or more providers, as is the case, for instance, with many JSTOR, Project Muse, and other aggregator titles. Some libraries, particularly those that shared an online catalog, decided from the outset to use separate records for each manifestation of an e-journal. This decision was more labor intensive but better than the alternative that would have made a mockery of the overburdened bibliographic record.

During the past few years, libraries have automated the record creation process. Brief bibliographic records can be derived using title lists provided by such e-journal aggregators as Expanded Academic Index. These records can be batch-loaded into the catalog, resulting in quick-and-dirty OPAC access to these titles. Acquisition of more descriptive MARC record sets is also a popular way to make the most of precious staff resources. Automated methods for adding e-journal lists to library Web sites have also been developed during the past few years, partly in response to the persistent debate regarding which access point is better—the online catalog or the Web site. By the end of the 1990s, database-driven Web lists of e-journals began to replace manually maintained pages. These databases can not only create dynamically generated Web pages, but by using such an application as MyLibrary, developed by Eric Lease Morgan, they can also create personalized Web lists. Both OPAC and Web site access to e-journals are valuable services provided by libraries.[10] Such link servers as SFX and course management software further exploit this medium.

Electronic Resource Management

Because libraries have developed useful protocols for providing e-resource access to their users, many libraries recently have begun to focus on the management of administrative metadata about these e-resources. Administrative metadata are elements about licensed electronic resources, such as the terms of a license, the name and contact information for a vendor representative, the purchase arrangement, and the URL where usage statistics are located. Administrative metadata are often filed away in a cabinet or an e-mail mailbox, or, to the chagrin of library managers, misplaced or even discarded. Libraries are now discovering just how important it is to provide access to these data.

Libraries have struggled for quite some time to organize the administrative elements associated with licensed resources. Even in the golden days, when e-journals were all free and when librarians did not have to create elaborate databases to manage them or lease nuclear-powered printers to reproduce their contents, it was clear that the day would come when the way users access electronic content would mature but that contracts, and the lawyers who write them, would make life hell forever.[11] As collections migrate from print to digital, and permissions—from those allowed through copyright to those dictated by a contract—are negotiated, it is increasingly important for librarians to understand the effects license terms have on their patrons' use of e-resources.

Electronic resources, especially electronic serials, offer many of the same challenges librarians have faced for years when dealing with print materials, but also offer a host of new ones. Libraries of all types and sizes purchase access to an increasing number of e-resources. These resources possess an array of restrictions, elements that don't easily fit, and were never intended for capture by ILS. Administrative metadata are increasingly needed by library staff in both technical and public services departments to answer questions such as how much money the library spends annually on electronic resources. What seems like a straightforward question is quite complicated to answer. For example, if a library purchases a print subscription to a journal for $1,000, and electronic access to the journal costs an additional $500, the payment is often posted to look as if the subscription was $1,500 and electronic access was included as a by-product of that fee. Many library systems have no way to distinguish between the amount spent for the print subscription and the amount spent for electronic access, but that distinction is very important when libraries are trying to obtain budget information for subscriptions being converted from a free-with-print pricing model to other pricing models.

In addition to providing access to e-journals and capturing the administrative details within the framework of an ILS, the elements important to managing electronic resources generally fall into three broad categories: licensing, purchasing, and administration. Licensing involves a myriad of terms that dictate how and by whom the resource may be used. Some of these elements include restrictions on interlibrary loan, remote access, use in course management tools, the number of concurrent users, archival access guarantees, and indemnification. Purchasing data include such elements as vendor name, expiration date, pricing model, and consortial arrangement. Administrative data include such elements as OpenURL compliance, availability and frequency of usage statistics, administrative passwords and documentation, and technical contact information.

By 1996, librarians recognized that managing licensing agreements would be more problematic than creating and maintaining Web links.[12] While few libraries did much to resolve this issue initially, it didn't take long before a handful of research libraries began building systems to help them manage administrative metadata. Some of these systems married the organization of administrative metadata with the delivery of e-resources to end-users. In this regard, these systems were unique. Although several libraries had created database-driven e-resource delivery systems by the end of the 1990s, only a few had also created the administrative piece. Three early systems that influenced later designs, as well as the standards currently under development, are MIT's Virtual Electronic Resource Access (VERA), Penn State's Electronic Resources Licensing and Information Center (ERLIC), and Johns Hopkins' Electronic Resource ManagEment (HERMES) systems.[13]

These three systems and the solutions they offered were described in considerable detail in a 2001 article by Nathalie Schulz.[14] From the description of these systems, it was obvious that the issues surrounding licensing were the most desperate and it was comforting to know that many libraries were facing the same challenges as those Schulz described.

The Electronic Resources Tracking System

The Tri-College Consortium consists of Bryn Mawr, Haverford, and Swarthmore Colleges, three small liberal arts institutions located within a ten-mile radius of each other in the suburbs of Philadelphia. The colleges have shared an ILS, Tripod, an Innovative Interfaces product, since 1990. Collaborative efforts during this time have grown steadily, especially with respect to consortial purchasing of electronic resources. These efforts are often time-consuming and challenging, to say the least, but they allow the three libraries to operate as if they were a larger institution with respect to both staff and budget. Electronic resource acquisitions within this small consortium are growing exponentially. Through the outstanding efforts of the Tri-College Consortium cataloging departments, the consortium is able to provide OPAC access to these e-resources, even those titles available through aggregator services. However, the ILS does not provide a means of recording the administrative elements associated with licensed resources. Traditionally, these data have been kept in paper files or as e-mail messages, which makes them difficult to resurrect or reconstruct when questions arise. Furthermore, the library system does not provide a mechanism for generating useful statistics about the electronic holdings. There is no way to tell how many e-journals are received as a consequence of print subscriptions versus how many are received based on the cost of the print subscription plus an additional fee. Prior to creating the Electronic Resources Tracking System (ERTS), the libraries struggled to identify when resources needed to be renewed.[15] Many resources expired at the end of the calendar year, others at the end of the fiscal year, and still others expired at various times throughout the year. Staff desperately wanted to know when these e-resource subscriptions expired before someone inquired why a publication that had been freely accessible suddenly required a username and password for access.

In early 2001, upon receipt of a Mellon Foundation grant, discussions about the state of e-resources within the consortium began and the idea for ERTS was born. The ERTS Team consisted of Haverford's coordinator, bibliographic and digital services, Swarthmore's head of technical services, Bryn Mawr's catalog and serials librarians, and the Tri-College Consortium's special projects librarian. Early in the development process a decision was made that the data to be tracked could be accommodated in one of four categories:

- licensors, entities from whom e-resources are licensed;
- vendors, entities from whom e-resources are bought;
- purchases, expenditures made to access e-resources; and
- titles, individual e-resource titles.

As a consortium, the Tri-College Consortium needed ERTS to reuse data and to accommodate up to four instances of unique data, one for each of the libraries and one for the consortium. For example, when a record for the e-journal *Astrophysics* is entered in the titles file, the licensor, Kluwer, is entered in the licensor file. Haverford buys the Kluwer collection through PALINET, which in this case is the vendor. Because each library has its own purchase arrangement with PALINET for the Kluwer collection of which *Astrophysics* is a part, each library also creates its own purchase record and is able to link to the shared title, licensor, and vendor records. ERTS has helped the libraries and consortium get control of e-resources in ways that just weren't possible before. It provides statistics that were not previously available as well as the ability to centrally retain all the data needed to manage the growing collection of licensed electronic resources.

Digital Library Federation Electronic Resource Management Initiative

The Digital Library Federation (DLF), through its Electronic Resources Management Initiative (ERMI), is developing a project to create standards for e-resource administrative metadata which all types and sizes of libraries will find useful for managing electronic resources.[16] This project is spearheaded by Timothy D. Jewell, head of collection management services at the University of Washington. After talking with librarians from a variety of libraries who were building tools to help them manage e-resources, he concluded that this was an area where communication among developers would be beneficial.[17]

E-resource Control

Providing free e-journal access to libraries that subscribed to a print version of a journal was a brilliant marketing move on the part of publishers. Unfortunately, libraries that turned their faculty and students into e-resource junkies can no longer bankroll their users' habits, due as much to the uncertain economy as to changing pricing models.

Nearly half of Haverford's serials budget is spent on e-resources, yet the library staff knows very little about these resources. This state of affairs exists in many libraries and should be of great concern to librarians. In the world of print serials, when an issue did not arrive in a timely fashion, the ILS issued an alert about the missing issue and the staff addressed the problem by issuing a claim for non-receipt of the item. In the world of electronic serials, users are often the first to discover problems pertaining to access to an e-resource and the first to alert the library about the problem. This scenario happens all too frequently and puts libraries in the unpleasant position of being perceived as poor custodians of these expensive resources. Librarians need to take back control of serials. The Tri-College Consortium is investigating the feasibility of importing serial notification data as a way of getting a little more information than is presently provided about the e-journal collections. The consortium is also looking at other aspects of the e-journal processes in an attempt to redesign them in ways that will eliminate redundancies and improve service to the users. How successful this project will be remains to be seen, but the time and effort spent investigating will certainly be worthwhile.

Conclusion

Richard Atkinson, formerly the president of the University of California, put it well when he said, "librarians are now being forced to work with faculty members to choose more of the publications they can do *without*."[18] Atkinson's comments were made in response to the ever-increasing subscription rates of scholarly journals. Weren't e-journals supposed to solve the serials pricing crisis? Unfortunately, the consequence of electronic publishing has not been to lower the cost of serials for libraries, but on the contrary, to increase prices well above their already high and unsustainable rates of growth. Part of the dilemma is due to the perception that e-journals are complements to, not replacements for, print journals. Although libraries are taking steps to migrate subscriptions from print to electronic when feasible, most maintain hybrid, content-duplicative serials collections. In order to realize the transformation to electronic-only collections, librarians need specific publisher guarantees, and more importantly, the blessing of faculty, many of whom have sentimental, albeit passionate, reasons for wanting to retain print journals. Life for librarians would be much simpler if publishers would cease their print operations entirely.

However, significant changes are taking place that may finally make a portion of the scholarly literature important to teaching and learning freely accessible. The open access movement is not a new concept. E-print servers in such disciplines as physics, computer science, and economics have existed for years. The Open Archives Initiative (OAI) was founded in 1999 to enhance access to scholarship in the growing number of e-print archives. Among OAI's greatest accomplishments is its Protocol for Metadata Harvesting, a mechanism for providing and capturing metadata about e-prints.[19] Theoretically, e-print repositories and a search and retrieval tool, such as the Protocol for Metadata Harvesting, could obviate the need for traditional publishing outlets if peer-review controls were in place.

In October 2003, the Public Library of Science (PLoS), a nonprofit organization of scientists and physicians, established such a model when it launched its first journal, *PLoS Biology*.[20] Three years in the making, the PLoS is a full-fledged scholarly journal publisher with an outstanding editorial team and a unique pricing model. PLoS journals are free—almost. Readers of the journals pay nothing; authors pay a fee of $1,500 per article to publish their articles—a fee the PLoS expects authors' institutions and other agencies to provide. To this end, the Wellcome Trust and the Howard Hughes Medical Institute announced that they would pay these fees for their researchers who publish their grant-funded work in open-access journals. That adds up to a few hundred million dollars per year for research results that may be available for free to libraries and the scholarly community at large. Not surprisingly, many commercial publishers are skeptical about the sustainability of an author-driven pricing model, reminding open-access proponents that PLoS was awarded a $9 million grant from the Gordon and Betty Moore Foundation, and that once the seed money is exhausted, $1,500 per article will not be enough to manage the costs associated with providing an electronic journal. It does seem clear, however, that open-access scholarly journals, especially those with editorial boards of the caliber of *PLoS Biology*, have a greater chance of being cited, and therefore of attaining a higher-impact factor within their field. Particularly in the sciences, faculty on the tenure track may be enticed to publish in a journal with a high impact factor, thus reversing the claim that freely available Web-based journals will never attract such scholarship. The open access movement is obviously exciting, at least from the librarian's perspective, but there are still many issues to be resolved, both technically and politically. In the meantime, there is plenty of work to do.

Converting this house of horrors into a comfortable home will not be easy. Electronic resources must be fiscally and administratively tamed. Libraries must develop processes that help them manage e-resources in efficient and realistic ways. An agreeable set of standardized license terms between libraries and publishers would be a good first step towards achieving this goal. A market ready to burst with ERM systems may help libraries redesign e-resource workflows and capture the data necessary to know more about these expensive, coveted resources. Rather than being marginalized, serials agents should repurpose themselves to provide useful tools and services that would empower libraries to control e-resources in ways similar to those used to control traditional print serials. Without effective management practices, electronic resources will run wild, and libraries will have no recourse but to watch the resulting destruction.

REFERENCE NOTES

1. C. Sumner Spalding, "Keeping Serials Cataloging Costs in Check," *Library Resources & Technical Services* 1, no. 1 (1957): 13–20.

2. Michael Gorman, "The Academic Library in the Year 2001: Dream or Nightmare or Something in Between?" *Journal of Academic Librarianship* 17, no. 1 (1991): 4–9.

3. John Cox and L. Cox, *Scholarly Publishing Practice: The ALPSP Report on Academic Journal Publishers' Policies and Practices in Online Publishing* (Rookwood, U.K.: John Cox Assoc., 2003).

4. Gail McMillan, "Electronic Journals: Access through Libraries," in Laverna Saunders, *The Virtual Library: Visions and Realities* (Westport, Conn.: Meckler, 1993), 111–29.

5. Steve Hitchcock, Leslie Carr, and Wendy Hall, "A Survey of STM Online Journals 1990–95: The Calm before the Storm" in *Directory of Electronic Journals, Newsletters and Academic Discussion Lists*, ed. D. Mogge, 6th ed. (Washington, D.C.: Association of Research Libraries, 1996), 7–32. Accessed 16 April 2005, http://journals.ecs.soton.ac.uk/survey/survey.html.

6. McMillan, "Electronic Journals."

7. Nancy B. Olson, *Cataloging Internet Resources: A Manual and Practical Guide* (Dublin, Ohio: OCLC, 1995).

8. James Holmes, "Cataloging E-journals at the University of Texas at Austin: A Brief Overview," *Serials Librarian* 34, nos. 1/2 (1998): 171–76.

9. Regina Reynolds, "Inventory List or Information Gateway? The Role of the Catalog in the Digital Age," *Serials Review* 21, no. 4 (1995): 75–77.

10. Formerly at North Carolina State University, Morgan has been head of the Digital Access and Information Architecture Department at the University of Notre Dame since 2001.

11. Tom Moothart, "Providing Access to E-journals through Library Home Pages," *Serials Review* 22, no. 2 (1996): 71–77.

12. Ibid.

13. Massachusetts Institute of Technology, VERA: Virtual Electronic Resource Access Web site, (Cambridge, Mass.: MIT Libraries, 2005). Accessed 1 Nov. 2005, http://libraries .mit.edu/vera; Johns Hopkins University, HERMES: Hopkins Electronic Resources ManagEment System Web site, (Baltimore, Md.: John's Hopkins University, 2005). Accessed 1 Nov. 2005, http://hermes.mse.jhu.edu:8008/hermesdocs/.

14. Nathalie Schulz, "E-journal Databases: A Long-term Solution?" *Library Collections, Acquisitions, & Technical Services* 25, no. 4 (2001): 449–59.

15. Additional information about ERTS, as well as its freely available source code is available at Tri- College Consortium Electronic Resources Tracking System Web site (Philadelphia: Tri-College Consortium, 2005). Accessed 1 Nov. 2005, www.haverford.edu/library/erts/.

16. Digital Library Federation, "DLF Electronic Resource Management Initiative" (2002). Accessed 16 April 2005, www.diglib.org/standards/dlf-erm02.htm.

17. In August 2004, the Digital Library Federation Steering Group issued its final report, *Electronic Resource Management: Report of the DLF ERM Initiative.* Accessed 1 Nov. 2005, www.diglib.org/pubs/dlfermi0408/.

18. Richard Atkinson, "A New World of Scholarly Communication," *Chronicle of Higher Education* 50, no. 11 (2003): B16.

19. Open Archives Initiative Protocol for Metadata Harvesting, Accessed 1 Nov. 2005, www.openarchives.org/OAI/openarchivesprotocol.html.

20. PLOS, Public Library of Science Web site. Accessed 1 Nov. 2005, www.publiclibrary ofscience.org/.

21. Steve Lawrence, "Free Online Availability Substantially Increases a Paper's Impact," *Nature* 411, no. 6837 (2001): 521.

Why Aren't Librarians More KISSable?

Keeping Electronic Resource Management User-centered

TIM BUCKNALL

What is it with librarians, anyway? Everyone knows that libraries are difficult for users to navigate, but it just does not seem possible to simplify things enough so that all users can find what they need without assistance. What is it about the KISS principle—keep it simple, stupid—that librarians do not understand? The answer, of course, is that librarians do understand the KISS principle—only too well—warts and all.

Take search interfaces for example. Librarians understand that patrons who master complex query systems will be rewarded with tightly focused search results. They also recognize that the majority of patrons prefer simple, easy-to-use interfaces, even if the search results are far from optimal. So when librarians consider designing user-centered information systems, they are faced with a dilemma. Is user-friendliness best achieved by a simple, Google-like interface that patrons say they want? Or is it user-centered to educate users—teaching them the best way to get the best results, even though they do not like having to learn something complicated?

Each definition of user-centered carries its own risks. It has been argued that adopting the simple, single search-box approach is the library's final capitulation to the trend towards mediocre, dumbed-down solutions, and that librarians have abdicated their role in educating information-literate, lifelong learners. In other words, encouraging patrons to use a simple system that yields lots of results with low relevance is not user-centered.

On the other hand, asserting that a nuanced and complex approach to information is better for users flies in the face of reason when they obviously

This paper is based on a presentation made at the ALCTS Midwinter Symposium "Taming the Electronic Tiger: Effective Management of E-resources," held in San Diego, January 2004.

prefer simple interfaces over increased search-result relevance—as witnessed by the fact that integrated library systems (ILS) see far more keyword searches than controlled vocabulary searches. Librarians must remember that library users have other options. Zealously ensuring that patrons use the best search methods, rather than the easiest, forces them to use a complex interface that is not to their liking. As a result, many users will no doubt opt instead to type www.google.com into the browser's URL field. An approach that drives many users away from the library's tools could hardly be considered user-centered.

Fortunately, resolving the definitional differences of user-centeredness is not necessary before real progress can be made in creating a truly user-friendly atmosphere. There are at least three things that libraries can do that will satisfy the proponents of almost any definition of user-centeredness:

> adopt an ecumenical approach to organizing and accessing electronic resources by using tiered and parallel access schema, which avoids sectarian arguments within the library community;
>
> look for simple improvements that benefit everyone, no matter how user-centered is defined; and
>
> adhere to a librarian's version of the Hippocratic oath and do no harm by removing anything that actively misleads library users.

Parallel or Tiered Constructions

One way to implement the KISS principle and maintain more powerful, complex approaches is by offering both parallel and tiered search capabilities. Tiered search options are more successful than parallel search options. For example, librarians would not consider placing both the brief bibliographic display and the full machine readable cataloging (MARC) record on the same screen at the same time. The short-and-sweet display comes first with a link to the richer detail. This allows users to self-select the level of complexity they prefer—an act of empowerment that seems inherently user-centered.

Libraries have followed this fairly simple principle for some time, yet it must be more fully implemented with regard to electronic resources. The following examples of information structures are overwhelming to users because they lack tiered or parallel construction.

Too Many Search Options

Given that many users prefer a simple Google-like approach, librarians should probably try to meet them halfway. Users have more success with subject searching through a keyword search feature than searching through Library of Congress Subject Headings (LCSH), a prominent option in most libraries that most users do not understand. Libraries would not, of course, want to entirely eliminate LCSH searching, but it could be moved to a less-prominent place on the user interface, thus emphasizing the much more useful (and user-friendly) author, title, and keyword search options. Experience has shown, for example, that LCSH are most effectively used by nonlibrarians as a "find another one like this" feature that locates related materials after the results of a keyword search have been retrieved. For example, few people looking for information on the Dred Scott decision would find it based on the arcane LCSH, "Scott, Dred, 1809-1858—Trials, litigation, etc," but almost anyone can locate information on that topic with the intuitive keyword search for "Dred Scott." That search retrieves numerous results with fairly high relevance, and users can then follow the LCSH hyperlinks in each MARC record to obtain other closely related works. Prioritizing search options and placing only the most essential ones in the most visible locations and keeping other options to less-prominent locations is one way to ease user confusion.

Another way to reduce search options is using metatools, which search many things at once. The trend towards metasearching has been very positive for most users. While it is true that these tools are somewhat dumbed-down, when correctly implemented, they supplement rather than replace the native interfaces of catalogs and commercial databases. With a tiered approach, libraries can offer simplified searching for those that want it, and complex searching for those who care to pursue it.

Too Much Metadata with Too Limited an Appeal

Effective tiered information displays would greatly improve the usability of library catalogs. Why should librarians show specific information to every user when only a few need it? For example, it is doubtful that many people care much about the ISSN (or as one recent questioner called it, the *issen*). It should be there for those who need it, but this specialized information can be safely removed from the brief bibliographic display and relegated to the seldom-seen full display, along with control numbers, LCSH, and descriptive information.

In addition, libraries could significantly improve the descriptions of their electronic resources. On many library Web sites, database descriptions are often long-winded and contain extraneous or even downright confusing information. For example, every library has a comprehensive alphabetical list of databases. An entry for the popular InfoTrac OneFile database on this list might say:

> Full-text database covering 1980 to present. Indexes about 8,000 titles cover-
> ing social sciences, humanities, science, and other areas.

How much of that do users really care about? Most users seem to see only "full-text." Portions of the description are misleading, such as "8,000 titles," all of which certainly don't go back to 1980, as the text implies. Do users know the difference between the social sciences and the humanities? Perhaps "general" could more succinctly describe the content. Boiled down to its essence, an adequate description for the vast majority of users would be

General. Includes full text.

The rest could be relegated to a linked information page where all the gory details are included.

Cluttered Homepages

Information on the library homepage, the front lobby of any virtual library, should be better organized. In a library building, things are clearly laid out so that when users enter they immediately see the most important services and signposts pointing them to the rest. Few libraries try to cluster almost all of their many services just inside their front door. But Web pages sometimes make it look like that's exactly what librarians are doing. By adopting a tiered approach and emphasizing services that interest the most users, librarians can create a more user-centered, less overwhelming, and more welcoming information environment.

Librarians can implement the KISS principle for those who want it and still preserve more advanced information and features. If electronic resources are correctly tiered, users will not be squirted in the face with a fire hose when all they want is a sip of water.

Simple Improvements

Today's librarians have to deal with an extremely complicated information environment that can sometimes prove completely overwhelming. If trained information professionals sometimes find this information environment to be more than they can handle, then it stands to reason that users will be even less able to effectively cope. Librarians cannot make everything easy for the user—it simply is not possible—but they can implement the KISS principle on a smaller scale by addressing minor, annoying issues and pursuing effective, limited solutions wherever possible.

Remove Extra Steps

Remove extraneous steps that add no value. Users are impatient—they expect to be able to get to things quickly and easily and have little tolerance for fancy splash pages. Worse are the hoops through which many remote users must leap before being granted access to paid resources. Standard proxy servers often require different, multistep set-up instructions for different browsers and even require different versions of the same browser. It is not clear why libraries persist with these methods when more transparent, user-friendly options are available at minimal cost. In fact, several products require nothing more than an ID number from users in order to log in.[1] Any librarian who has to teach frustrated users how to configure a browser to access the library proxy server should definitely look for more patron-centered options.

Clarify Categories

Make categories readily understandable. When electronic resources were introduced in libraries, simple alphabetical finding lists sufficed. After all, there is not much to be gained from subdividing half a dozen databases that can be displayed on a single screen. But with the proliferation of electronic resources, there is a clear and urgent need to improve the way users are directed to the information they want. Users simply do not want to be confronted with Web pages that list hundreds of items. However, when it comes to dividing these pages by subject, there is no consensus on what level of subjects are most user-centered. Some libraries use very narrow, specific headings while others employ much broader ones.[2] Beyond subject divisions, things get less clear. Splitting resources into free and paid categories is popular, but why do libraries do that? Does the mere fact that PubMed is free somehow make it intrinsically different from commercial versions of MEDLINE? Does the user even care whether the library pays for something or not? Users only care about what's free and what's paid if they are the ones expected to do the paying. In a similar vein, many libraries juxtapose the terms database and Web site, usually a restatement of the paid versus free distinction. That probably leads to even greater confusion for users. Aren't both PubMed and MEDLINE databases, and aren't they both on the Web?

Follow the User

Make the system match the user's behavior rather than trying to make the user match the system's behavior. Creating a user-centered system means building it in such a way that its use is completely clear to the user, so that ideally the user would never have to ask for help. That goal would not be achieved for some time (and if it is, it may put librarians out of work), but some strides can be made in that direction. Instead of telling a user he or she is doing it wrong automatically, why not build services to identify incorrect use and instantly correct it?

Intelligent systems that learn user behavior may sound like science fiction but are available today. For example, at the University of North Carolina at Greensboro (UNCG), Journal Finder (a locally developed OpenURL link resolver and knowledge base) logs all searches that retrieve no hits. Once the library staff obtained a large enough data sample, user queries were reviewed and analyzed and it was discovered that, as anyone who works the reference desk could have predicted, users repeatedly make the same mistakes when searching for serial literature. After analyzing the actual mistakes, library staff wrote corrective algorithms that made the search tool automatically identify and correct the incorrect search behavior in real time as patrons queried the system. Some of the changes to title searching were fairly obvious, such as dropping initial articles and normalizing "and" and "&." Other changes were less obvious. For example, subtitles were automatically dropped from all searches because actual usage data clearly showed that doing so would improve retrieval accuracy. The same log file is used to teach Journal Finder how to better meet the needs of its users. For example, "close enough" titles are added to the database as added titles (analogous to the MARC 246 $$a field), so that the system learns from its mistakes. Thus, when a user searched for "News Week" and got no hits, staff figured that the title (incorrect though it is) was close enough and should have retrieved "Newsweek." In this manner, the system was adjusted so that close enough forms of a title could be retrieved. Now users can find the correct journal title even if their search contains initial articles, errors in the subtitles, or nonstandard abbreviations or titles. After all, users certainly do not care whether they are searching the correct way—they just want correct results.

Make It Obvious

Put what users are looking for where it can be easily found. The Web is the primary access mechanism by which users reach electronic resources. Making these resources truly user-centered means that librarians have to make sure electronic resources are easy to find through the library Web site. Because information-seeking behavior varies among users, there is no one, perfect place where these resources can be located so that they are universally available. Instead, links for electronic resources need to be put in all the places that users are likely to look for them. At UNCG, for example, the library Web site has approximately 5,000 links that will lead a user to EBSCO Academic Search Elite. More than 2,000 of these links go directly to individual journal titles from the catalog and another 2,000 link from the library's link resolver and knowledge base to the journal title. The Academic Search Elite database is linked from the library's alphabetical list of databases, from the catalog, from subject lists of databases, from subject lists of e-journals, from individual class resource pages (e.g., English 101), and from many other avenues, including even special-purpose Microsoft Word documents. There is no way all this could be manually maintained—this type of approach requires automated solutions. At UNCG, the many links to Academic Search Elite all use a single Perl script to connect to the target resource and to route users through a proxy when appropriate. As a result, changes to the database uniform resource locator (URL) only need to be made in one place rather than in 5,000 places. Macros have also been written for the ILS (DRA Web2) to create an appropriate automatic pseudo-856 link whenever a patron views a serial record in the catalog. No fuss, no muss, and no need for catalogers to maintain 856 field links.[3] Librarians must create ubiquitous links throughout library Web sites to ensure that users can find and access electronic resources—the most rapidly growing portion of many library collections. To maintain their sanity, librarians must create solutions. There is no way librarians can keep up with tens of thousands of links manually.

Use What Works

Find popular and successful features elsewhere and emulate them. Most library users do not use the library exclusively—they use a variety of online resources to obtain electronic information. It makes sense for librarians to look at the competition and see what attracts users to other sites. This is not to say that librarians should emulate every single innovation by Google, Yahoo!, and Amazon.com. Rather, they should evaluate what is being done successfully in other markets and decide whether similar features could be implemented successfully and would satisfy users. For example, although they lack substance, the convenience of Amazon.com's book reviews is remarkable. At UNCG, staff were able to take the best aspects of the Amazon reviews and improve on them with macros and OpenURL linking to establish automatic links from the bibliographic records to the appropriate reviews in InfoTrac OneFile. These reviews are much more objective and critical than their Amazon.com counterparts and they further enhance and leverage a relatively expensive resource (InfoTrac). If library users think a particular feature is user-centered in an external environment, then they will probably think it is user-centered if libraries adopt it as well.

These issues do not, of course, constitute a comprehensive list of things libraries can do to make electronic resources more user-centered. A list derived by one library might be completely different than one derived by another. Nevertheless, the lists should all share a common theme: that decision-making, organization of information, and system development should be centered on the needs of the user. That is easier said than done given that librarians don't necessarily agree on what constitutes a truly user-centered approach. At the very least, librarians would probably agree that misleading users cannot be considered user-centered.

Misleading the Users

Few libraries seek to deliberately mislead their users, but users are mislead almost every day. The complexity of academic, public, and commercial institutions and the variety of their resources will always cause misunderstandings. Libraries should, however, attempt to minimize misleading users. An ongoing evaluation of library services should yield an in-depth understanding of users' information-seeking behavior and would be a key to this problem.

User Expectations

Tools should behave the way patrons expect them to behave. Of the innumerable examples, a common problem involves searchable lists of electronic journals. This type of tool usually contains a search box and a browsable list of titles beginning with each letter of the alphabet. An informal usability test found that most patrons chose the letter rather than filling in a title in the search box. In other words, if they were looking for "The Journal of Zoology," they would click on "J" (or, more likely, "T") rather than type the title into the search box. When asked why they did that, every single user had the same answer: "it's faster." The only problem with that answer is that it is wrong. Clicking on letter "J" is faster than typing in the title, but the library at UNCG, for example, has more than 5,000 titles that begin with "J." Once the titles are retrieved, it takes a long while to scroll or page to the desired title. During the test period, more than 80 percent of the cases showed that retrieving a title through typing into the search box was faster than clicking on initial letter first. Consequently, it is probably best not to offer features that behave counter to users' expectations.

Expecting Users to Know Something They Do Not

Sometimes libraries lead patrons down a virtual blind alley and abandon them there, rather than giving them directions on how to get where they want to go. For example, for a search for a journal to which the library does not maintain a subscription, an incredibly nonhelpful result screen would say "Your search for xxx retrieved no results," which leaves users with the impression that the article they need is not available. A much more helpful response would be a "No titles that match your search were found" message that includes a link to ILL or document delivery. In this way, patrons will realize that the article they need can be obtained. More helpful messages can be quite easily arranged and will probably not result in an explosion in ILL requests.

Deliberately Misleading

Unfortunately, libraries occasionally deliberately mislead users. For example, pay-per-view services are frequently omitted from the library catalog. When libraries make that decision, users searching the catalog for a pay-per-view journal will be told, in effect, that the library does not have access to that title.

To be truly user-centered, an information system not only has to meet users' needs but also must perform according to the users' expectations. If electronic resources are organized and presented in other than expected ways, patrons will be misled, which is hardly the basis for a user-centered system.

Assessment

How do librarians know where libraries are on the path to establishing a user-centered environment and how will they know when the goal has been achieved? A regular assessment program can ensure that the library's electronic resources meet user needs and expectations. Most libraries gather data to evaluate electronic resources and services in one of three ways, each of which has pros and cons.

Gathering Opinions

Asking users how to make accessing electronic resources easier is not uncommon, but it is not as prevalent as one might expect. So whom do the librarians always ask? Each other, of course. The rationale is that the librarians work closely with users and are thus best positioned to decide what users need. The rationale ignores some rather obvious biases.

In their interactions with the public, librarians do not necessarily deal with either a statistically significant or a random sample of the user population, which may skew their perceptions of users' needs. Library staff may sometimes grossly exaggerate the issues that they personally wish to have resolved. For example, a frustrated staff member may indicate that a particular technical problem occurs many times every day and thus has to be immediately fixed. In fact, log files actually show that this technical problem occurs much less frequently than claimed.

Anecdotal evidence and opinions often reflect what people think they want and not what they actually use. For example, a survey was conducted in UNCG's Jackson Library to ask students if they would use chat reference if the library implemented such a service. A majority of those sampled said they would use it, but when the service was initiated, only a tiny percentage of the student body used it. In this case, there was an enormous difference between what users said they would use and the reality of what they actually used.

Despite the inherent flaws of opinion-based data, it is important that the library staff and the public be involved in evaluation and assessment. Gathering opinions is a great place to start data collection, but it is a terrible place to finish it.

Quantitative Analysis

As a whole, librarians do not believe in sampling. They feel compelled to count every database access, every reference question, and every book circulation. This data is used to justify a library's existence by proving that the staff is indeed serving users.

That same data can be used to make decisions about which services have the highest priority. For example, if users are flocking to e-journals and the use of printed journals is in decline, collection developers might want to consider buying additional e-journal packages. The greatest benefit of this approach is that priorities can be based on what people actually use, as opposed to their opinion of what they might use in the future.

The chief problem with this approach is that it measures only the quantity of use and ignores the quality of use. For example, Web log files could reveal that an electronic books page is the most frequently visited page on a library's site. From that statistic, staff might infer that people love the e-book collection and think the service is wonderful. Yet the numbers do not actually say that. It may be that users are looking for the library catalog and click on an "electronic books" link because they think it is a way to find printed books. Or they may be looking for specific e-books and not finding them. Or they might find exactly what they want, but then get frustrated by trying to read or check the item out online. Quantity of use should not be directly equated with user satisfaction. Usage data is generally underused in decision making. It is great when combined with opinion or usability data, but it can be misleading in isolation.

Usability Data

In a typical usability test, the library gives a small group (usually five to seven people) specific tasks and observes them to see what problems they encounter. For example, to test the efficacy of their lists of electronic resources, a library could bring in a representative group of users and have them use the library's electronic resources to find the difference between a crocodile and an alligator or to find an article on securities fraud at Enron. As the testers navigate the Web site, they are encouraged to give a running commentary on what they are doing and why. The result provides fascinating insights into the motivation behind user's behavior. For example, one person said, "I'm choosing the database EBSCO Masterfile because it is the Master and must have the most info."

These tests yield excellent qualitative data that help librarians determine whether the Web site is being effectively used. They can show success rates for each task and tallies of how many times people clicked before they were successful (or gave up in frustration). Librarians can also get direct data on why users clicked on the links they selected. This not only enables staff to target the most misleading and problematic areas of the Web site, but also may provide direction for improving those areas.

Surveys and opinion gathering are used most often but are least effective, while usability testing is the most effective assessment tool, but it is used most infrequently. It is worth noting that none of the assessment methods work well in isolation. Identifying and developing user-centered approaches to a library's electronic resources requires a holistic approach to assessment mechanisms and a balance between the penchant for quantitative data and data that measures the quality of users' interactions with libraries.

Conclusion

Librarians may not agree on the definition of user-centered, but they can certainly agree that there are many aspects of the KISS principle that can be implemented to make electronic resources meet the needs of users in a more satisfactory manner. Now that there is significant competition from Google and its peers, it is crucial that librarians enhance and improve the user experience sooner rather than later. If librarians want to maintain their central role in the information-seeking process, they must take less pride in mastering complex systems and more pride in making the inherently complex systems simpler and more inviting for library users.

REFERENCE NOTES

1. The most widely used of these products is EZ Proxy. Accessed 16 April 2005, www .usefulutilities.com.
2. UNC–Greensboro has used the institution's academic departments as subject headings—Math, English, Dance—and that seems to be something to which users can easily and effectively relate.
3. Readers can see how this works by going to http://library.uncg.edu and searching the catalog for a serial. When viewing a serial record, an apparent 856 field link will be visible to the Journal Finder knowledge base that, on closer examination of the MARC record, is not an 856 field at all. Accessed 16 April 2005.

Taming the Tiger Technologically

Through the Standards Jungle (and out Again Unscathed!)

FRIEDEMANN WEIGEL

The concept of electronic information is built on a multitude of standards. The process of accessing a piece of electronic content involves the implicit usage of more than a hundred, if not hundreds of standards of some sort. Standards are ubiquitous in providing, accessing, and managing electronic resources. Navigating the standards jungle requires a road map. The road map model may not be entirely appropriate in this context because it suggests that the issue is simply getting from point A to point B. A more complex model that not only describes the core components of the environment, but also expresses the major relationships and interdependencies of the components would be better. To continue the analogy, finding a way out of the jungle is not the only task—understanding how to traverse the jungle in any direction is also required. Or, as Outsell reports in a 2004 briefing for the information marketplace "XML [(extensible markup language) is] freeing content from the documents and archives that bind it. Our industry is not on some linear path toward an ideal state or equilibrium, but rather is moving on multiple, fragmented paths to an unknown but bigger future."[1]

At the 1997 IFLA meeting in Copenhagen, an early map (model) for electronic resource management (ERM), similar to figure 1, was unveiled. It listed the major aspects of ERM:

1. *Content*—the raison d´etre of the industry

2. *Access*—the way to get to the content

3. *Acquisition*—a reflection of the underlying business processes

This paper is based on a presentation made at the ALCTS Midwinter Symposium "Taming the Electronic Tiger: Effective Management of E-resources," held in San Diego, January 2004.

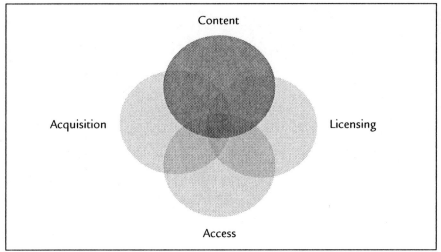

FIGURE 1
ERM Model 1

It is interesting to note that at this relatively early stage of e-content development there was no mention of the issue of licensing electronic resources. In the last several years, however, the focus has shifted from the technically oriented theme of content provision toward service-oriented issues, such as acquisition and licensing. The model in figure 1 is strong and beautiful because it is very precise, and even though at first glance the model looks simple, it is really quite complex. This complexity is expressed in the number and the characteristics of the points of intersection.

A somewhat more elaborate version of the same diagram contains additional details about the core components. See figure 2.

In this model, identifiers and metadata characterize each of the core components and take the place of the core intersection. Preservation has been added as an element of content, and usage and authentication as components of access. This model is by no means final; in fact, the intersections need further refinement. However, it would be helpful if the information community could agree on this or a similar generalized model or concept for ERM while simultaneously working on some of the many details it entails.

Another useful way of looking at ERM was developed by R2 Consulting and was introduced at the 2003 Charleston Conference.[2] This model considers ERM from the library's perspective and is highly function- and workflow-oriented. See figure 3. In this model, ERM is broken down into nine distinct components, which in the long run will help libraries and others to be well-positioned to accept such standards as online serials exchange (ONIX) for serials and EDItX/EDI.

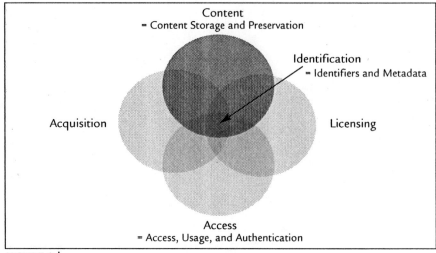

FIGURE 2 | ERM Model 2

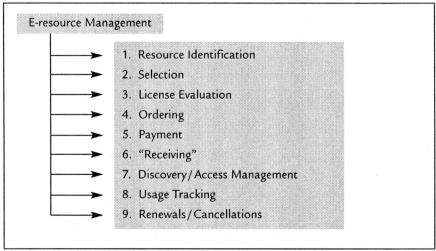

E-resource Management

1. Resource Identification
2. Selection
3. License Evaluation
4. Ordering
5. Payment
6. "Receiving"
7. Discovery/Access Management
8. Usage Tracking
9. Renewals/Cancellations

FIGURE 3 | ERM Model 3

While the components proposed in figure 3 have considerable potential for ERM, the major players in the field are more comfortable with a more general model that incorporates the major standards in use today.[3] See figure 4.[4]

In this model, the technical standard for content provision is ISO 8879:1986, better known as standardized general markup language (SGML). The beauty of SGML is that a document can be maintained once but published in multiple media. Hypertext markup language (HTML) and extensible

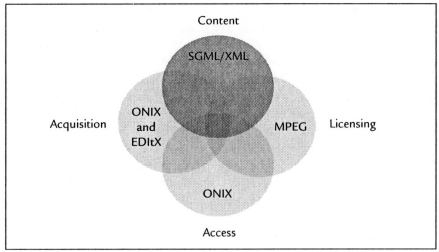

FIGURE 4 | ERM Model and Relevant Standards

markup language (XML) are both SGML applications. Extensible markup language, although still in its infancy, having been on the scene for only half a dozen years or so, has been fully embraced by the World Wide Web Consortium (W3C). Several features of XML make it very powerful:

- it uses Unicode, which gives it global usability;
- it is platform independent and browser enabled;
- it can describe complex data not just by supplying structured containers for content but also by providing the means to describe the role of the content of these containers; and
- in contrast with HTML and traditional EDI standards, such as UN/EDIFACT and ANSI X12, which incorporate syntax and semantics, XML is simply a form of grammar and does not provide for any predefined tags.[5]

Tagging is part of the document-type definition (DTD) or schema-building process and therein lies the problem. If publishers would focus on developing a common full-text XML DTD (and schema), they could avoid a great deal of the complexity—which consumes a lot of time and money—as so many publishers are shifting to XML.

XML seems to be the means of taming the tiger. It is not just the technological platform for content description and provision—the cradle for electronic journals in a sense—XML is also very likely the base technology for the storage (and certainly for the exchange) of descriptive and management data about electronic resources. In this context it is also appropriate to mention Adobe's portable document format (PDF) as a *de facto* standard tool for content provision, the Digital Library Federation's Electronic Resources Management Initiative (DLF ERMI) developments for metadata standards for preservation, as well as the Lots of Copies Keep Stuff Safe (LOCKSS) initiative for preservation and archiving.[6]

A number of groups are developing standards for licensing agreements and those developments are probably underrated. The Moving Picture Experts Group (MPEG), ISO/IEC 18034, is responsible for developing a standardized rights expression language (MPEG-21 Part 5) and a rights data dictionary (MPEG-21 Part 6). "A rights expression language is seen as a machine-readable language that can declare rights and permissions using the terms as defined in the rights data dictionary."[7] The U.S.-based Open E-book Forum (OEBF) is also developing a publishing extension to the MPEG rights expression language.[8] Less technical and considered to be more a code of practice is the sample license promoted by the Association of Subscription Agents (ASA) and originally designed by John Cox Associates.[9]

Wouldn't it be wonderful to have a common license that is acceptable to many publishers, so librarians and their lawyers don't have to review and negotiate each one? And wouldn't it be nice to have a uniform way to size an institution and count use while usage-based and tiered-pricing models take hold? This may very well be the crux of the problem. It is quite surprising that there is so little comment or discussion within the industry about what would appear to be exciting and promising developments.

ONIX is one of the major standardization developments for supporting access, and although it is often thought of as a toolset for the acquisition process, there is much more going on in the access arena including:

- the Open Archive Initiative for creating a meta index that can be used by service providers to extract metadata from data providers[10]
- the OpenURL ready to be approved as National Information Standards Organization (NISO) standard Z39.88(2004) (the metadata schlepper)[11]
- Project Counting Online Usage of Networked Electronic Resources (COUNTER) for harmonizing the usage of electronic content[12]
- Shibboleth for supporting the concept of a single sign-on[13]

With regard to such identifiers as the international standard serial number (ISSN), serial item and contribution identifier (SICI), digital object identifier (DOI), and CrossRef, the most interesting development seems to be the redesign of the ISSN.[14] One of the core questions is whether the ISSN should be the same or different for various expressions and formats of the same content. Two proposals are now under discussion: one suggests that all versions of a journal (electronic, paper, microform) should carry the same ISSN, not different ISSNs as is presently the case, and the other recommends that different formats of a journal be identified by a suffix to the ISSN, set by the publisher, which would not form part of the registered ISSN. The outcome of this process is open, although chances are that the work that has been done on revising the ISSN is in danger of faltering due to the high and possibly rather diverse, if not disparate, needs and expectations of the various players in the production, distribution, and consumption chain for serials.

Acquisitions is the final component of the ERM model. In the ILS environment, the acquisition process makes use of such standards as the European Book Selector Electronic Data Interchange Group (EDItEUR) message suite for serials, including electronic data interchange (EDI) claims, claim responses, invoices, and dispatch advice.

Understanding the present environment with regard to the management of electronic resources requires some background information. The situation facing the information industry today is very similar to that of the 1970s before machine readable cataloging (MARC) or the 1990s before EDI when libraries, publishers, and vendors were on the verge of significant changes in their business practices. A brief look back is useful for getting an idea about the impact and consequences of what was then perceived as a major standardization activity. The paper-based supply chain cycle is a classic example. See figure 5.[15]

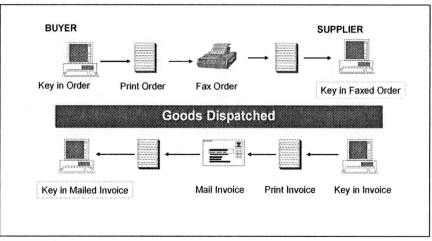

FIGURE 5

Traditional Paper-based Supply Chain Cycle (source: 2002 e.centre)

In this typical supply chain process from the 1970s, the buyer produces an order by keying the relevant information into his local system, printing it, transmiting it by mail or fax to the supplier, who receives the paper copy of the order and keys the information into the suppliers' local system. Producing an invoice follows a similar process: keying, printing, mailing, keying again.

National and international standards, such as United Nations/Electronic Data Interchange for Administration, Commerce, and Transport (UN/EDIFACT) helped to reshape the business cycle so that format interrupts during the workflow, such as changing from one medium to another, were reduced to a minimum. Rekeying information could be totally avoided, business processing became primarily automated, and the processing speed of the entire business cycle was dramatically improved. Figure 6 illustrates how enhanced network connections and the exchange of standardized machine-readable information were the key elements of this development.[16]

Wonderful, it works! Hurray! So, why can't ERM be accomplished by implementing a couple of standards addressing ERM issues? There are a number of reasons why this seemingly straightforward approach is not appropriate for the management of electronic resources. Thirty years ago, the journal as a business concept was stable, well understood, and had existed largely unchanged for many years—a business model in cement! That type of business environment could easily accept new standards and could be replicated in an EDI structure. Today, however, the underlying business structure of acquisitions is less stable and not understood very well, making the development and subsequent introduction of standards more complex and challenging.

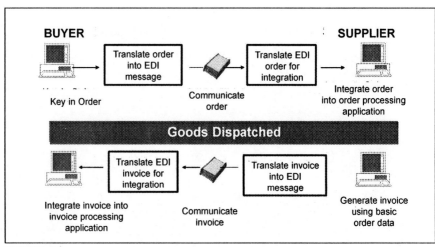

FIGURE 6 | EDI Applied to the Business Cycle (source: 2002 e.centre)

When considering new standardization ventures, lessons from the introduction of other standards (e.g., EDI) can be helpful. Disconnects exist between the designer, the implementer, and the user of the message (standard). This may be a result of a breakdown in communication between the members of the information chain (supplier, ILS vendor, library) and a misunderstanding about the amount of time required to develop, test, and implement the standard. For example, X.400 technology could easily have been adopted, but communication difficulties have allowed the Internet to completely overshadow and outperform the technology. Reducing redundancy in a message is a time-consuming task. There are often many ways of expressing the same idea—getting all the players to agree on simplifying procedures and eliminating or reducing redundancy is often difficult because communities of interest tend to hold on to outdated procedures. Figure 7 shows how well such standards as EDI work for the big players (e.g., Fortune 1000), but shows that they are not nearly so satisfactory for small and medium-sized businesses (SMEs).

Today's situation is different in two specific areas. SGML with its Internet orientation no longer acts solely as a supporting network but now serves as an incubator for open technology. There are more types of players and fewer players per market segment, resulting in a much more diverse and highly multifaceted marketplace.[18] See figure 8.

The enormous variations in pricing, licensing, formats, and packaging options for content need to be addressed by and reflected in developing standards by creating a mainstream business model for e-content. How do standards fit into this picture? To a large extent, the old standards continue to work in the

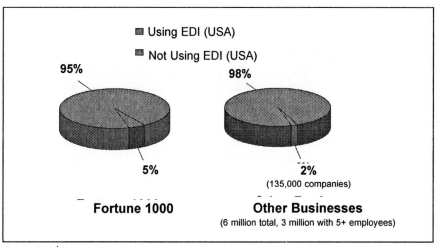

FIGURE 7
EDI in the U.S.: Fortune 1000 versus SMEs (source: 2002 e.centre)

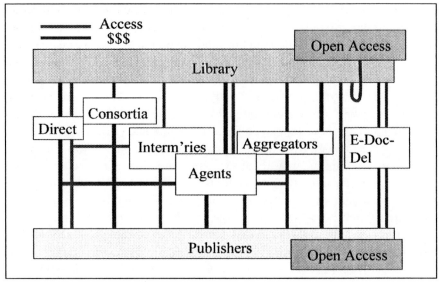

FIGURE 8 | Acquisition and Access Process (source: ASA, Rollo Turner)

area of acquisitions. The UN/EDIFACT-based EDItEUR message cycle for serials works very well for electronic resources. This message cycle must be revised to include additional e-resource specific elements and a migration of the semantic definitions from EDIFACT into XML—what is now referred to as EDItX. When it comes to licensing and access issues, however, there is still a huge vacuum in the practical application of standards and the focus is no longer on content but on service. Fortunately, there are significant developments taking place in the area of service. Coincidentally, the development of the ONIX for Serials message suite has caused great anxiety in this area.

ONIX for serials is a structured, comprehensive, extensible metadata standard for journals and other serial resources. As an evolving group of messages designed to support specific business needs in the serials sector, it is a sibling of the widely used ONIX for books standard, with which it shares both an approach and a data dictionary. ONIX is based on XML with applications validated and controlled by either schemas or DTDs. It was developed and is hosted as an open standard by EDItEUR and maintained as a result of close interaction with international user groups. At present, ONIX for serials supports three message formats:

- serial online holdings (SOH)
- serial products and subscriptions (SPS)
- serial release notification (SRN)

The serial online holding message was designed by the EDItEUR/NISO Joint Working Party Public Access Management Systems (PAMS) to Libraries Subgroup.[19] It supports the communication between libraries and their hosting and access management services for their online resources and helps to populate resolution servers with information on resources subscribed, completeness levels, and e-formats. The given XML schema basically supports two main exchange models a flat, A–Z listing of online resources and the same set of information but grouped by hosting services. In collaboration with the DLF ERMI initiative, work is underway to enhance coverage of license terms and conditions. In a typical library application, SOH data will be used to build and update the local A–Z list.

The serial products and subscriptions format is a development of the EDItEUR/NISO Joint Working Party Agent/Publisher to Library Subgroup. The addressees of this message are libraries interested in finding out about the complete range of resources available from publishers, particularly e-journal access rights derived from paper purchases and their pricing. It also addresses publishers who want to assemble a more complete picture of library holdings, directly or through intermediaries. The ONIX SPS format has been devised to support three options:

- a list of serial products available on subscription from the sender, showing the works and versions of works contained in each;
- a price list of the serial products; or
- a list of serial products with prices for a particular subscriber, including current prices and prices last paid.

A typical application for a library would be the electronic transfer of a list of the library's subscriptions.

The serial release notification format for article- or issue-level exchanges also consists of three parts:

- the serial title record;
- the serial item record; and
- the subscription package record.

This format is used to describe serial publications, their parts, and their product variations. Conceivable exchanges include article metadata sent to abstracting and indexing services, document delivery, library and hosting services, metadata for DOI registration, and structured TOCs.

Figure 9 suggests that there is at least one standard for each workflow component. *Cum grano salis!* More pilot projects and implementations are needed

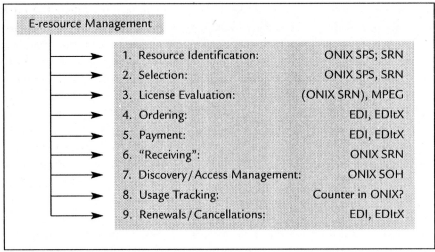

FIGURE 9 | ERM Model 3 and Applicable Standards

before it will be possible to say that all phases of ERM workflow are covered by appropriate standard messages. A good start has been made with the standards that support each activity and the flexibility of these new messages, which can accommodate quite a range of functionality.

Standards consist of two components: a meta language and a business model. The language—powerful XML derivatives such as ebXML or ONIX is ready for use.[20] What continues to lag behind is an acceptable business model. All segments of the industry are beginning to feel the pressure and, as a result, the impetus to look for solutions exists. Relief is not quite available, but it is coming. A number of mapping projects are being developed. One should keep in mind, however, that standards will only work with excellent technical support and maintenance and the wholehearted participation of all the parties involved. Pilot projects—lots of them—are needed. Although EDItEUR, NISO, and such library-driven initiatives as DLF ERMI provide an efficient framework for further development and maintenance, more active membership and participation of all parties involved is needed in order to more rapidly advance this development.

Conclusion

Powerful technical standards for the management of electronic resources are available and are being used in pilot projects. XML-based ONIX is at the core of this development. The underlying business or distribution model is unstable, which makes it a moving target for any kind of standardization concept. A proliferation of standards makes it difficult to identify and enforce best practices. In the absence of the five-hundred pound gorilla in the information industry (e.g., Wal-Mart in the retail industry), strong support and participation from all the interested parties is needed to form best practices, codes of conduct, and wise shopping attitudes. Standards, ONIX in particular, will make life easier: the tiger can be tamed technologically.

Taming a tiger means taming a predator. One of the great American horsemen, Pat Parelli, has found that horses, prey animals, "do not care how much we know until they know how much we care."[21] Adopting this healthy attitude means that we must pay attention to how much the business partners care while we define new business models and practices for the precious commodity of information and content.

REFERENCE NOTES

1. "InfoAboutInfo Briefing: Outlook 2004, *Issues in the Information Marketplace*" 6, no. 32 (Dec. 19, 2003): 4. Accessed 16 April 2005, www.outsellinc.com/outlook.

2. Rick Lugg and Ruth Fischer, "Agents in Place: Intermediaries in E-journal Management," (Contoocook, N.H.: R2 Consulting, 2003). Accessed 16 April 2005, www.ebookmap.net/pdfs/AgentsInPlace.pdf.

3. EDItEUR Web site (London, U.K.: Editeur, 2005). Accessed 16 April 2005, www.editeur.org. Standards are completely documented and available, including ONIX for Books, ONIX for Serials, ONIX Code Lists Version 2 (for all ONIX formats), EDI Implementation Guides, EDItX XML EDI Document Formats, and FTP File Naming Conventions.

4. W3C, "Overview of SGML Resources" (Cambridge, Mass.: MIT, 2005). Accessed 16 April 2005, www.w3.org/MarkUp/SGML/; W3C, "Extensible Markup Language" (Cambridge, Mass.: MIT, 2005). Accessed 16 April 2005; www.w3.org/XML/; W3C, "HyperText Markup Language (HTML) Home Page" (Cambridge, Mass.: MIT, 2005). Accessed 16 April 2005, www.w3.org/MarkUp/; W3C, "MPEG Pointers & Resources" (Cambridge, Mass.: MIT, 2005). Accessed 16 April 2005, www.mpeg.org/MPEG/index.html; EDItEUR, "EDItX XML Document Formats," (London U.K.: EDItEUR, 2005). Accessed 16 April 2005, www.editeur.org.

5. UNECE (United Nations Economic Commission for Europe), United Nations Directories for Electronic Data Interchange for Administration, Commerce, and Transport Web page. Accessed 29 October 2005, www.unece.org/trade/untdid/welcome.htm; Accredited Standards Committee (ASC) X12 Web page. Accessed 29 October 2005, www .x12.org/x12org/index.cfm.

6. Adobe, "What is Adobe PDF?" (San Jose, CA: Adobe) Accessed 29 October 2005, www .adobe.com/products/acrobat/adobepdf.html; Digital Library Federation. "A Web Hub for Developing Administrative Metadata for Electronic Resource Management." Accessed 29 October 2005, www.library.cornell.edu/cts/elicensestudy/home.html; LOCKSS (Lots of Copies Keep Stuff Safe) Web site. (Palo Alto, Calif.: Stanford University). Accessed 29 October 2005, http://lockss.stanford.edu/.

7. Organisation Internationale de Normalisation, ISO/IEC JTC1/SC29/WW11, "Coding of Moving Pictures and Audio," 5.5 MPEG-21 Part 5—Rights Expression Language; 5.6 MPEG-21 Part 6—Rights Data Dictionary. Accessed 29 October 2005, www.chiariglione.org/mpeg/standards/mpeg-21/mpeg-21.htm.

8. International Digital Publishing Forum Web site (formerly Open E-book Forum) (New York, N.Y.: DPF). Accessed 29 October 2005, www.idpf.org.

9. "Model Standard Licenses for Use by Publishers, Librarians and Subscription Agents for Electronic Resources" (John Cox Associates, Towcester, U.K.). Accessed 29 October 2005, www.licensingmodels.com; ASA, Association of Subscription Agents and Inter-mediaries, (Rollo Turner, High Wycombe, Buckinghamshire, U.K.). Accessed 29 October 2005, www.subscription-agents.org.

10. Open Archives Initiative Web site. Accessed 29 October 2005, www.openarchives.org/.

11. NISO Committee AX Web site, "Development of an Open URL Standard." Accessed 29 October 2005, http://library.caltech.edu/openurl/.

12. COUNTER, Counting Online Usage of NeTworked Electronic Resources Web site. Accessed 29 October 2005, www.projectcounter.org/.

13. Internet 2, Web page Shibboleth® Project (Ann Arbor, Mich./Washington, D.C.). Accessed 29 October 2005, http://shibboleth.internet2.edu/.

14. Library of Congress, National Serials Data Program, US ISSN Center. Accessed 29 October 2005, www.loc.gov/issn/; Berkeley Digital Library SunSITE, "SICI : Serials Item and Contribution Identifier Standard." ANSI/NISO Z39.56-1996 Web page, Version 2. Accessed 29 October 2005, http://sunsite.berkeley.edu/SICI/; International DOI Foundation (IDF), The Digital Object Identifier System (DOI) Web page. Accessed 29 October 2005, www.doi.org/; Crossref Web site. Accessed 29 October 2005, www.crossref.org.

15. GS1 U.K., (London, U.K.) GS1 UK became the new name for e.centre in February 2005. e.centre was the trading name of the Association for Standards and Practices in Electronic Trade—EAN UK Ltd—which was launched in October 1998 after the merger of the Article Number Association (ANA) and the Electronic Commerce Association (ECA). Accessed 29 October 2005, www.gs1uk.org/.

16. Ibid.

17. GS1 U.K., "SME = Small and Medium-sized Enterprises." Accessed 29 October 2005, www.gs1uk.org/.

18. Rollo Turner, "Agents and Intermediaries: The Jam in the Sandwich" (High Wycombe, Buckinghamshire, U.K.: Association of Subscription Agents and Inter-mediaries, 2003). Accessed 29 October 2005, www.subscription-agents.org/papers/Charleston 2003_2.ppt.

19. NISO/EDItEUR Joint Working Party for the Exchange of Serials Subscription Information. Accessed 29 October 2005, www.fcla.edu/~pcaplan/jwp/sub_pams.htm; NISO, "Exchanging Serials Information." Accessed 20 October 2005, www.niso.org/news/SerialsExchange.html.

20. Electronic Business using eXtensible Markup Language (ebXML) Web site, (Billerica, Mass.: Organization for the Advancement of Structured Information Standards). Accessed 29 October 2005, www.ebxml.org.

21. Pat Parelli, "The Seven Games of Parelli Natural HorseManShip," VHS. (Rackenford, U.K.: Savvy Centre, 1994).

Making Sense of User Statistics

First the Bad News

ROBERT MOLYNEUX

The tide of the information revolution sweeps everyone along with exciting promise as nifty digital tools
reduce the cost of producing and disseminating information. The bad news is that collecting data with
these new digital tools is difficult. The good news is that the tools for measuring
usage statistics are steadily improving and one completely new tool is being introduced. Measuring the use of electronic and traditional materials is one of the
most complicated issues facing librarians as they engage in budget and policy
discussions.

In her survey "Use and Users of Electronic Library Resources," Carol
Tenopir refers to studies "on how people use electronic resources or on their
feelings about electronic and print resources in the library," suggesting correctly
that both quantitative and qualitative elements must be considered when gathering usage data.[1] Of particular interest are quantitative elements that have
proven difficult to analyze.

Since 1995 the U.S. National Center for Education Statistics (NCES)
under the Federal-State Cooperative System (FSCS) has collected data on electronic resource expenditures by individual public and academic libraries, but
there is no consistent data on electronic resource usage.[2] In the academic
library community, studies that gather information on the cost and use of electronic resources are conducted by the International Coalition of Library
Consortia (ICOLC) and the Association of Research Libraries (ARL). These

This paper is based on a presentation made at the ALCTS Midwinter Symposium "Taming
the Electronic Tiger: Effective Management of Electronic Resources," held in San Diego,
January 2004.

studies are fairly well-known, while similar efforts within the public and state library communities are less well-known but no less intense.[3] In addition, there are no readily available, consistent, national-level statistics on consortia spending for electronic resources or the use of electronic resources in the consortial environment.

What Are Usage Data?

Studies on how people use libraries predate the computer. In theory, at least, quantitative usage data should now be easy to obtain because they are automatically generated and stored in computer system transaction logs. In practice, however, usage data have not only been difficult to collect and extract, but even more difficult to analyze. This occurs, in part, because attitudes about electronic resources are not easily quantified and definitions of what is being observed are not as precise as they need to be. As a result the data are open to interpretation: information is garnered from surveys or interviews or inferred from data in log files. For instance, how does one count a click or a double click? How much time elapsed between the two clicks? What if the second click is merely the result of an impatient user? Should the click be counted once or twice?

Direct quantitative-use measurements of physical resources have always been difficult to obtain. Measuring the usage of a journal volume is a good example of this problem. A common method of use measurement simply consists of keeping track of the number of times a volume of a journal is reshelved — a straightforward procedure, except when library users reshelve volumes themselves. To counteract this behavior, which would lower the resultant numbers, librarians conducting such studies often ask users not to reshelve volumes, which in turn may lead to additional complications.

Some usage studies, such as Paul Metz's 1979 work, "The Use of the General Collection in the Library of Congress" are well-known and well-constructed. Unfortunately, these early use studies tend to be episodic and there are not enough of them to gain much more than heuristics about the way people interact with library materials.[4] Librarians have come to believe that past use of materials is a reasonable indicator of future use, although predicting future use with any confidence of accuracy or validity is not realistic. These early studies also make it clear that information on the use of materials is skewed by discipline, type of library, or class of borrower, with the result that these heuristics are not very reliable for purposes of planning collection development or budgeting, except in the most casual way. This characterization of usage studies is not meant to denigrate their value but rather to point out how complex the task of data collection is and how many variables can impact the results. It is a testament to the pioneers who carried out these early investigations that they now serve as a foundation upon which contemporary studies are being built.

Context

Recent library data provide significant details about library size and the cost of providing services and collections, but they provide very little information on how collections are actually used or what value they have to the community. In addition, there is a desperate keenness and urgency for usage data about electronic resources that does not manifest itself when measuring other more traditional aspects of library services and collections.

The cost of providing library services continues to increase while library budgets decline. At the same time, institutions are under tremendous pressure to maintain access to electronic resources. Librarians must point out to administrators and decision-makers the importance and value that users place on electronic resources to ensure that decision-makers support the acquisition and licensing of electronic resources and the development of reliable data collection tools.

Measuring Use

Measuring use is an extremely difficult task, even with computers. Data are naturally elusive. In measuring the use of library materials, change occurs so rapidly that even establishing definitions is problematic. Agreement on definitions is vital because standards cannot be developed without it. Definitions must remain stable for a long period of time in order to minimize misunderstandings during and after data collection. Data collection professionals know that different interpretations of the definitions and different methods of collection can distort data the first time they are collected. After the data collection period, it is common to find that some data were either never collected or were not accurately or uniformly collected. Only by collecting data for an extended period of time can one gain confidence in the accuracy and validity of the data and therefore feel secure that the definitions have been vetted. This does not mean that useful conclusions cannot be drawn from data collected during the early stages of a project. Rather, those using the data should be aware that as definitions stabilize and data categories are solidified, fewer anomalies will appear in a data set.

Another problem facing data compilers is the length of time it takes to implement data collection after an agreement on the definitions has been reached. In the print environment, using manual data-collection tools, it is not unusual to experience a lag of several years between the concept for the data collection and the actual collection of the data. In the electronic environment, using automated data-gathering processes, data collection should be much more efficient, particularly once the definitions have been determined. Nevertheless, the fact remains that the electronic materials themselves and the usage-measuring tools are changing faster than the data-collection processes can accommodate.

The extent to which libraries have been able to obtain standard usage data continues to be problematic, and will likely remain so until questions about the definitions are resolved. There has been little consistency in how vendors and publishers measure usage or what criteria they have used to obtain their measurements. The number of hits counted by one vendor might reflect the number of items downloaded from a resource, while for another vendor it might indicate the number of items found as a result of a search. Some vendors count downloads of material in hypertext markup language (HTML) format separately from downloads of portable document format (PDF) documents, while other vendors may group the two formats together. In addition, vendors tend to measure different things for different periods of time, and the resulting data are frequently incomparable. As long as there is no consistency in the way vendors measure and output usage information, it will be difficult to determine which resources offer the best value. Yet, in the world of data collection and analysis, it has often been necessary to compare apples and oranges. Metz and Cosgriff, in their study "Building a Comprehensive Serials Decision Database at Virginia Tech," demonstrated how incomparable data could be used satisfactorily. While their methods were sensible, they were also complex.[5]

A further complication in the data collection and analysis effort stems from the fact that vendor contracts often do not allow individual libraries to share their usage data. In a presentation at the Charleston Conference in 2003, Phil Davis advocated creating a "publicly available, distributed database where libraries are able to share with other libraries price, usage, and other information about deals reached with publishers."[6] Davis argued that such a national database would ultimately result in both transparent pricing models and in a large and meaningful corpus of data that libraries and consortia could use to gauge their own costs and usage against those of their peers. At least initially, developing such a database is complicated by that fact that many vendors do not allow libraries to publicize either their costs or their usage data, and therefore the database would be limited to those institutions whose contracts are free of these restrictions. Ultimately, if vendors realize that this information will not negatively impact their ability to market their product, this concept may gain acceptance.

The lack of substantive usage data may also be traced to a second fundamental problem: there are not enough researchers trained in the quantitative analysis of library data. Quantitative data are generally used either to support decision making or for research purposes. While it may seem that these two concepts are mutually exclusive, they normally work in concert. Individuals who understand how to conduct research will gather better data and better understand the relationship between research methodologies and data gathering and analysis. As a result, they can create data that better supports decision making. Unfortunately, librarians have avoided using data to support decision making as a transition to using data for research purposes because the number of librarians trained in quantitative analysis and dedicated to measuring, collecting, and analyzing library data historically has been very small.

The practical implications of this reality are that the use of data in the library field is neither sophisticated nor broadly based. A number of excellent data series exist, such as the public library series from the NCES's FSCS— recently recompiled into a longitudinal series at the National Commission on Libraries and Information Sciences (NCLIS)—and the data from the ARL which go back to 1907–08, but too few librarians have the expertise to provide meaningful analysis of the data.[7] Summary statistics show that more than $14 billion is spent every year on libraries, but no qualitative measures exist to help librarians understand whether that money is being spent wisely.[8] Are the electronic resources provided by libraries the ones on which they should be spending their money? It would seem that difficulties in measuring electronic usage are very similar to the difficulties encountered in measuring other activities, services, or collections.

Now for Some Good News

Despite the somewhat gloomy picture surrounding the collection of usage data for electronic resources, some indicators signal an improvement in the way electronic resources are measured. However, there is still hard work ahead.

Counting Online Usage of NeTworked Electronic Resources (COUNTER) grew out of Publisher and Librarian Solutions (PALS), a U.K. initiative that involved librarians, publishers, and vendors concerned with common problems.[9] The work of this group led to COUNTER, where the producers and the purchasers of electronic resources work together to develop consistent methods for measuring, collecting, and exchanging usage information about electronic resources. Since its inception, Project COUNTER has developed the "Code of Practice for Journals and Databases" and the "Code of Practice for Books and Reference Works."[10] Although drafting these codes was complicated and time-consuming, their adoption is proving to be a turning point in the analysis of electronic usage data. These codes "[provide] guidance on data elements to be measured, definitions of these data elements, output report content and format, as well as [assistance] on data processing and auditing. To have their usage statistics and reports designated 'COUNTER-compliant' vendors must provide usage statistics that conform to the code of practice."[11] After some initial resistance, the first COUNTER-compliant reports from individual institutions are now available through a number of vendors and publishers and represent significant progress in data generation. Now that the process has started, librarians should be encouraged that information sharing between institutions will occur as additional releases to the codes of practice are introduced.

One of the more interesting aspects of the codes of practice is that they provide for auditing of vendor reports to certify that the reports are COUNTER compliant. The auditing process was designed to be straightforward, without placing an undue burden or additional cost on vendors. If it works as anticipated, COUNTER-compliant reports could very well provide librarians with the most accurate usage statistics currently available.

Vendors are beginning to adhere to the standards developed by Project COUNTER. Reports are being issued in extensible markup language (XML) format so that libraries, including those where the staff has limited experience with statistical reports, can manipulate and analyze the data they receive. In order for Project COUNTER to be successful for the long term, publishers and aggregators must continue to provide strong support, demonstrate a willingness to share the usage data they gather with their customers, and allow these data to be shared between institutions both locally and nationally. Meanwhile, electronic resources management (ERM) tools that integrate many pieces of the serials puzzle are also being developed and will, in time, also include COUNTER data.

While Project COUNTER gains acceptance in the publisher and vendor communities, a number of consortia and large academic libraries are conducting independent research on the use of electronic resources. OhioLINK and the University of Pennsylvania have distributed reports based on usage data from their online resources.[12] While information gathered by these and other groups may seem to be of little relevance to librarians in smaller institutions or those who are not consortium members, observations about the statistical characteristics of use will provide a framework for other libraries or consortia that might be interested in replicating these studies locally. These large studies give librarians an opportunity to understand the problems institutions face when gathering and analyzing usage data, and they offer librarians ideas about collecting and analyzing data in other institutions or environments.

The most significant development with regard to data collection is that groups of individuals are expressing an interest in data analysis and the skills required for it. COUNTER involves librarians and vendors (itself a significant development), who are prepared to continue to work in this area even if other data-gathering endeavors should fail.

New tools are constantly being developed to provide more detailed and sophisticated data about the use of electronic resources. One such venture is the Normative Data Project (NDP) for Libraries, developed by the GeoLib Program at Florida State University and the Sirsi Corporation, a "cooperative effort by hundreds of libraries and leading library community organizations throughout North America [which will] compile transaction-level data from public libraries throughout North America; . . . link library data with geographic and demographic data; and . . . empower library decision-makers to compare and contrast their institutions with real-world industry norms on circulation, collections, finances and other parameters."[13]

After the data are collected, they are stripped of institution-specific information and grouped into common categories for comparison across libraries. When linked with demographic data from the GeoLib project, the NDP will provide sophisticated and detailed data on the hitherto poorly understood interaction between people and libraries. A project such as NDP has profound implications for decision-makers and is now possible because of the development of massive storage capabilities.

The Road Ahead

Much still remains to be done in the area of electronic resource data collection and analysis, particularly when the following interests of different groups are often in conflict:

> Librarians consider using the data to identify and cancel subscriptions for seldom-used materials, while aggregators and publishers anticipate using the data to add value to their existing services.
>
> Library patrons want easy access to information, preferably without coming to the library. However, there are often substantial costs involved in providing that access, so difficult decisions must be made whether the access achieved is worth the cost.
>
> Scholars in academic institutions have become sensitive to the price of periodicals, databases, and online resources, and have begun advocating alternatives to paid subscriptions, such as the Public Library of Science, an open source initiative, to replace well-respected and expensive periodical subscriptions.[14]
>
> Vendors wonder whether they can bypass libraries altogether by marketing and selling information directly to users.

Dealing with information at the user level raises major concerns about both trade practices and privacy. If users were able to buy information directly from publishers, publishers could track what users are reading. This practice could lead publishers to charge different rates for access to information, based on the knowledge obtained from tracking the use patterns or research habits of specific individuals or categories of users. This raises the question: is it necessary or even desirable to gather so much data and how much data transparency is reasonable?

In the end, the conundrum for librarians is the lack of an analytical community to examine the data that is presently available and that will become available in the future. In the past, librarians have relied on analysts from other disciplines to help evaluate programs, collections, and services. However, these analysts seldom have a strong background in or knowledge of library operations and procedures, and because their loyalties often lie elsewhere, they usually return to their home fields once the projects are completed.

Ultimately, as more and more data is gathered and reported, better analysis will be required, and as a new generation of librarians with the requisite analytical, quantitative, and leadership skills enters the profession, the expectation is that the situation will improve.

REFERENCE NOTES

1. Carol Tenopir et al., *Use and Users of Electronic Library Resources: An Overview and Analysis of Recent Research Studies* (Washington, D.C., Council on Library and Information Resources, 2003), iv. Accessed 2 November 2005, www.clir.org/pubs/reports/pub120/contents.html.

2. U. S. Department of Education, National Center for Education Statistics Web site. Accessed 18 April 2005, http://nces.ed.gov.

3. International Coalition of Library Consortia (Hartford, Conn.: Yale Univ. Library, 2005). Accessed 2 November 2005, www.library.yale.edu/consortia; Association of Research Libraries, "ARL Announces: Results Published from E-Metrics Study," (Washington, D.C.: ARL, 2002). Accessed 2 November 2005, www.arl.org/arl/pr/emetrics_study.html.

4. Paul Metz, "The Use of the General Collection in the Library of Congress," *The Library Quarterly* 49 (Oct. 1979): 415–34.

5. Paul Metz and John Cosgriff, "Building a Comprehensive Serials Decision Database at Virginia Tech," *College & Research Libraries* 81 (July 2000): 324–34.

6. Philip M. Davis, "Fair Publisher Pricing, Confidentiality Clauses, and a Proposal to Even the Economic Playing Field," *D-Lib Magazine* 10, no. 2 (Feb. 2004). Accessed 18 April 2005, www.dlib.org/dlib/february04/davis/02davis.html; "Fair Pricing, Information Asymmetry and a Proposal to Even the Playing Field" in *Charleston Conference Proceedings 2003* (Westport, Conn.: Libraries Unlimited, 2004). Accessed 18 April 2005, http://people.cornell.edu/pages/pmd8/fair_pricing_speech.doc.

7. U.S. National Commission on Libraries and Information Science, "*Enhanced Longitudinal Public Library Data File (PLDF3).*" Accessed 4 November 2005, http://nclis.gov/statsurv/NCES/pldf3/index.html; Association of Research Libraries,

ARL Statistics (Washington, D.C.: ARL, 2005). Accessed 4 November 2005, www.arl.org/stats/arlstat/index.html.

8. R. R. Bowker, *Bowker Annual of Library and Book Trade Information, 2003* (New York, R. R. Bowker, 2003).

9. Project COUNTER: Counting Online Usage of NeTworked Electronic Resources, (Edinburgh, U.K., COUNTER, 2005). Accessed 4 November 2005, www.projectcounter.org/.

10. COUNTER, "Code of Practice for Journals and Databases, Release 1" (Edinburgh, U.K., COUNTER, Jan. 2003); COUNTER, "Code of Practice for Journals and Databases, Draft Release 2" (Edinburgh, U.K., COUNTER, Apr. 2004); COUNTER, "Code of Practice for Journals and Databases, final version" (Edinburgh, U.K., COUNTER, Mar. 2005); COUNTER, "Code of Practice for Books and Reference Works, Draft Release 1" (Edinburgh, U.K., COUNTER, Jan. 2005). Accessed 4 November 2005, www.projectcounter.org/code_practice.html.

11. COUNTER, "Code of Practice for Journals and Databases, foreword," (Edinburgh, U.K., COUNTER, Mar. 2005). Accessed 4November 2005, www.projectcounter.org/code_practice_r1.html#section1

12. Ohio Library and Information Network. Accessed 4 November 2005, www.ohiolink.edu; Joe Zucca, "Find a Way or Make One: Strategies for Measuring and Analyzing the Use of Digital Information," PowerPoint slides from the ALA Annual Meeting in Toronto, June 20, 2003. Accessed 18 April 2005, www.arl.org/stats/newmeas/emetrics/arljune2003.ppt.

13. Normative Data Project for Libraries. Accessed 4 November 2005, www.library normativedata.info; Florida State University, Institute of Science and Public Affairs, Florida Resources and Environmental Analysis Center. Geolib. Accessed 4 November 2005, www.geolib.org.

14. PLoS: Public Library of Science Web site. Accessed 4 November 2005, www.plos.org.

Usage Statistics at Yale University Library

A Case Study

JENNIFER WEINTRAUB

In traditional all-print collections, librarians were generally satisfied with a relative understanding of how much the materials in their collections were used. Usage information was obtained by keeping records of the number of times materials were borrowed or reshelved. Sometimes studies were conducted to determine which journals were used for browsing; at other times information about level of use was gleaned by taking a cursory look at how worn or damaged the printed materials were or even how much dust had accumulated on them.

Usage statistics have been an essential factor in developing printed collections, and librarians need the same kind of data to help them develop electronic collections. In the electronic environment, librarians no longer have the physical clues to provide information about the use of purchased materials. Without vendor statistics, the best usage data that most librarians can expect to get is how many times users have connected to a database from a particular page on the library's Web site during a specific period of time.

Almost from the time that the Yale University Library began to collect electronic journals, the need for usage data was recognized, and since 1996 usage statistics for electronic resources have been actively collected and maintained. In the past, vendors and publishers used to fax or mail usage data to the library, but today vendors frequently make usage statistics available on the Web, retrievable by the library as needed. This article examines the kinds of usage statistics that the Yale University Library collects from vendors, the way the data are processed, the problems faced in gathering and maintaining usage statistics, and what the library ultimately hopes to gain from maintaining and analyzing this information. It also provides a snapshot of some of the current problems with collecting and maintaining usage statistics in many academic libraries.

Background

Subject selectors at Yale use many criteria when selecting resources, such as quality of content, authority, breadth, quality of electronic interface, and price of the resource. The subject and language coverage of the traditional print collection is wide and varied, and the library's electronic resources mirror that heterogeneity. Although Yale acquired a few electronic resources in the early 1990s, the acquisitions program for electronic resources only began in earnest in 1996, when the library first licensed a number of Web-based indexes to periodical literature. Since that time, a variety of materials, including electronic journals, electronic reference works, and electronic databases aggregating indexes to periodical literature and linked full-text, have been collected and with them, usage-related statistics have been obtained. More recently, as collections of electronic books have been acquired, usage statistics on those collections have also been obtained. As the library undertakes projects to digitize local collections and materials, statistics on their use will also be maintained.

At Yale, each journal or journal package is selected and acquired based on its own merits.

When a resource overlaps more than one subject, selectors work together to make a selection. If the resource is of broad general interest, it is considered by the Committee on Digital General Electronic Resources (CoDGER) and items selected by CoDGER are purchased from a central fund rather than from individual subject-area funds. The electronic collections unit manages the acquisition and maintenance of all electronic resources. This unit ensures that licenses are negotiated and signed correctly and provides information to selectors to help them make their decisions and to support them when selecting a resource. The unit also activates journal subscriptions and initiates renewals both with large vendors and vendors whose resources are funded by more than one selector. The electronic collections unit also collects and manages usage statistics, deals with any problems that might arise, and alerts selectors about pending renewals. Selectors evaluate and recommend electronic resources for Yale, while the electronic collections department handles the actual acquisition and renewal decisions.

Statistics Collected by Yale University Library

The Yale University Library has a broad view of usage statistics for electronic resources because it purchases and subscribes to thousands of electronic resources. While the library requests usage statistics from all its vendors, it only collects such statistics for approximately 25 percent of the licensed electronic resources. Although the number of vendors that supply usage data has grown each year as more vendors realize the importance of usage data and develop methods to track and supply that information, many of the library's vendors are small publishers still in the process of developing the capability to capture and transmit this information.

The selectors at Yale, working closely with the head of electronic collections, negotiate licenses for electronic resources. Every licensing agreement includes a requirement for the provision of usage statistics. If the vendor produces usage data, it is accepted, regardless of format.

Usage statistics are collected to:

>   monitor access to resources that have a limited number of simultaneous users and determining whether the number of users is accurate or needs to be adjusted;

>   watch for changes in usage that might signal access problems;

>   assess the value of materials to library users because the pricing and features of the library's resources fluctuate from vendor to vendor;

>   help in the decision-making process when evaluating two similar products that offer different interfaces or that cover different publications;

>   understand the information-seeking habits of users (while being careful not to invade their privacy), selecting appropriate resources, and designing useful services; and

>   understand how resources are used in conjunction with link resolvers and other linking technology, such as observing whether usage of a particular resource increases once SFX is implemented.

While usage statistics are an important component in the decision-making process, selection and retention decisions are not based solely on usage statistics. Resources with low usage may be retained if they contain unique materials that are important to a particular program or if they support ongoing research of specific laboratories or initiatives. As is the case with most major research library collections, most of Yale's print materials are infrequently used but are meant to provide great depth and breadth. In this way, Yale's electronic resources mirror its print collection. Subject selectors also use a variety of other criteria when recommending resources, such as quality and authoritativeness of the content, the quality of the electronic interface, and last but not least, the price of the resource.

How Yale Processes and Uses Statistical Data

The technological capabilities and sophistication of Yale's vendors of electronic materials vary considerably, as does their willingness and ability to provide usage data. As a result, there is a significant variation in the quality and quantity of the statistics the library receives. With nearly a decade of experience in acquiring and licensing electronic resources, the staff now has substantial experience with analyzing usage statistics, in particular for periodical indexing databases.

The way statistical data has been presented and disseminated for Yale's resources continues to dramatically change. Rather than receiving statistics by fax or through the mail, as was the practice some years ago, usage statistics are often available online. Many vendors and publishers provide customers with special passwords so that authorized individuals can access, review, and download the data. Yale prefers that usage statistics be located on the publisher's server and available through IP authentication, much the same way libraries access databases. This enables staff to look at the data without having to manage a special administrative password. In some cases, when statistical data is not available online at the publisher's or vendor's Web site, it may be provided in the form of a comma-delimited file attached to an e-mail message.

The electronic collections unit maintains a central Web page (available only to authorized users) with links to Yale's statistics.[1] See figure 1.

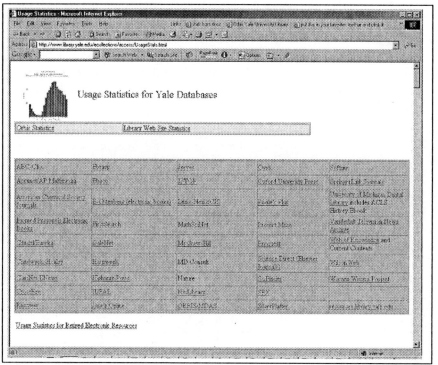

FIGURE 1
Yale University's Statistics Page

Some of the links go directly to statistics at the vendors' sites, some require passwords, while others are directly accessible based on IP authentication. If the statistics are not available from the vendors' sites or are too complicated to easily access, the digital collections specialist and the electronic collections assistant gather the usage data and create tables and graphs (first in Excel and then converted into hypertext markup language [HTML]) for posting on the Web where selectors and others can view them. See figure 2.

Not all usage statistics are provided to selectors: data is usually limited to one or two specific aspects of a database, such as the number of searches or citations. If more in-depth information about a specific resource is needed, selectors may request assistance from the electronic collections unit.

Maintaining statistics in a readable format on a library Web site is helpful because it offers everyone, including users, firsthand information about the use of a specific resource. Depending on the format in which the statistics are received, libraries may wish to manipulate them, extract data, or convert relevant data into Excel or some other appropriate format. Displaying statistics in graphical form allows users to visualize patterns of use that might otherwise be difficult to discern.

Given the large number of databases and electronic journal packages that are monitored, processing usage statistics has become an enormous task. Accumulating statistics for thousands of resources is extremely time consuming because of the massive amount of data, as well as the variety of formats and data points that must be handled. For instance, statistical data reported for databases

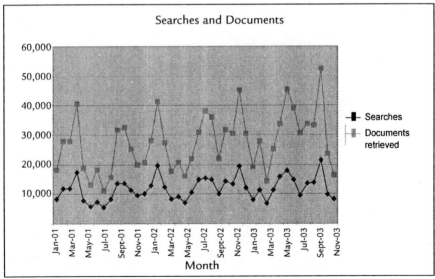

FIGURE 2 | Example of Graph Created from Vendor-supplied Statistics

typically includes the number of sessions, number of searches, and number of citations retrieved during a specific period of time. If Yale's license for a particular database is restricted to a specific number of simultaneous users, data would be provided concerning the number of users unable to connect when that limit was reached. The statistics generated for electronic journals may be different than those for databases and might include such data as the number of downloads per title in HTML, number of downloads per title in portable document format (PDF), number of tables of contents viewed, number of abstracts viewed, and occasionally, for such journal packages as ScienceDirect, the number of searches. In addition to the various types of statistics provided, the formats in which the data come also vary. HTML, text, or Excel formats are all used, depending on the vendor. While all of these formats are readable, some are not flexible enough to allow analysis of data for an extended period of time.

With the increasing availability of electronic books, Yale is beginning to gain some first-hand experience with usage statistics for these materials as well. Usage statistics for e-books include rankings of the most popular titles, activity by title, activity by subject, and number of turnaways (i.e., the number of users who could not access the material due to restrictions on the number of simultaneous users). While these kinds of data are not substantially different than those captured and reported for electronic journals, the difference lies in how librarians view e-book statistics. Most electronic books are bought in packages rather than individually so statistics are generally examined for a group of books according to a specific subject area or topic, rather than for an individual e-book title. As libraries begin to acquire and license other forms of electronic resources, such as statistical data sets, geographic information, and art and photographic images, new questions about effective ways to represent usage of these materials will begin to emerge.

In short, the usage data Yale receives is rarely uniform and thus not readily comparable. Creating reports that are useful to selectors based on that data is a highly complex, individualized, and labor-intensive activity.

Problems of Gathering and Maintaining Usage Statistics

As electronic resources have changed and grown in complexity, the statistics being collected have changed, particularly with regard to the amount of information available. Initially, libraries settled for rather basic information, such as the number of hits on a Web page. Now, after several years of experience with electronic resources and a higher level of sophistication among users, libraries expect and are often able to obtain data of much greater granularity, such as number of articles downloaded from a journal and the number of citations retrieved from a database. In fact, many of Yale's most popular general-interest resources now provide the most useful statistics. However, problems with both format and content of usage data remain, especially with smaller or developing products.

The statistical data themselves often engender confusion. Some vendors send only hits on a database or views of an electronic journal, a statistic that is virtually useless without a definition of hits or views. Is every image brought up in a browser window, such as a logo, being counted, or is only relevant data, such as the number of citations, being counted? Some vendors produce unsatisfactory statistics and still others irregularly produce statistics or are inconsistent about what is counted. In cases such as this, the library staff must work with publishers and vendors for help in interpreting the data. While frustrating and time consuming, these types of interactions with vendors or publishers can have a positive side—to raise awareness of the need to gather and provide standardized usage data in a systematic manner. Communication with vendors about statistical reports is an ongoing process. In 2003, Yale librarians answered at least five surveys about electronic resources, each of which included questions regarding usage statistics. These surveys were typically sent to the subject selectors and included questions about content, features, interface improvements, and pricing. Questions about the kind of statistics that would be most useful were often referred to the digital collection specialist. Yale's librarians take advantage of every opportunity to convey the library's requirements to vendors and their experience indicates that many vendors understand the need for meaningful statistics and are receptive to suggestions for enhancing their statistical products. Nevertheless, librarians have found that in some cases a significant amount of time must be spent managing passwords and handling error messages in order to effectively manipulate the statistics. In addition, errors or problems with data gathering can cause vendors to interrupt the provision of data or necessitate that statistics be sent again.

In terms of content, when vendors provide information on sessions, the kind of data provided may be different because data-collection protocols widely vary. For example, an article in one database or package may include editorials and letters, while another database or package may exclude editorials (or letters) from counts. Without standard definitions, comparing statistics from different resources is extremely complicated and unreliable, like comparing apples and oranges or trying to get an accurate count of electronic journals.

In addition to the diversity in format and content of statistics, another issue facing libraries is the amount of time required to effectively maintain statistics. While collecting and maintaining usage statistics is important, it is not the highest priority among the many tasks related to electronic resource management (ERM). It is clearly more important for library staff to make sure patrons can access all the electronic journals offered than to pursue electronic journal usage statistics for every resource. Unless a library has unlimited staff or a good supply of conscientious student workers, it can be difficult to keep up with even the relatively limited number of electronic resources that do provide statistics. Staff time is an important consideration when deciding how best it should be invested when analyzing usage statistics.

If usage statistics are gathered and maintained on a regular basis, they will be available whenever an electronic resource needs to be evaluated. Typically, when a decision about a resource has to be made, the data is needed immediately and the data should be organized and maintained in a flexible format so that it can be output on demand in a variety of ways, a goal towards which Yale is still striving. Statistics should be reported in an easy-to-understand format that allows for visual interpretation using graphs or charts and that readily lends itself to comparing data whenever possible. If this can be accomplished, the time-consuming task of assembling large amounts of data in response to urgent requests is much less stressful and more satisfactory for all parties concerned. However, based on Yale's experience, statistics will only be regularly gathered and maintained in such a flexible way if it is easy for libraries to do so.

Yale Library's Future Goals for Usage Statistics

Yale has participated with other libraries and vendors in efforts aimed at standardizing electronic usage data. This occurs in several ways. First, librarians clearly and frequently communicate with vendors. Second, between 2001 and 2003 Yale participated in the Association of Research Libraries (ARL) E-Metrics project.[2] The goal of that project was to adopt new measures for counting electronic resource use as a component of the annual ARL statistics. Yale also hoped that the project would encourage libraries and publishers to enter into discussions about standardizing statistics. Participants in the ARL E-Metrics project tested various statistical measures designed to capture usage of electronic collections. Although new questions were added to the ARL Supplementary Statistics in 2003–2004, unfortunately, there was no agreement about how use of electronic resources should be counted.

For libraries hoping for a breakthrough with regard to standardization of usage statistics the work of Project COUNTER and the COUNTER Code of Practice seem to offer the best hope for success.[3] Project COUNTER is supported by many publishers and vendors and is addressing the question of collecting and presenting statistics in a unified manner in order to improve the efficiency of data analysis. An exciting development from COUNTER is the possibility of gathering statistics from a number of vendors and producing a single report. As part of its code of practice, COUNTER has also attempted to standardize definitions so that it will be easier for libraries to compare and understand statistical information from different sources. COUNTER may decrease the overall variety of statistics received from vendors, but those statistics that it does provide will be in a standard format and use standard definitions of key measures. COUNTER's success will enable Yale and other libraries to more effectively analyze their usage statistics.

Because usage data for electronic resources is not available for all of Yale's e-resources, it is currently impossible for the library to produce an accurate, comprehensive usage report. As a result, special reports of usage statistics are often produced on demand. The most popular reports are those done by subject (e.g., history journals) or by format (e.g., databases). These prove useful when staff are preparing departmental reports or when bibliographers or selectors need special information about an academic program or department.

To better manipulate data in the future, usage statistics will be entered into a data farm, a database that enables greater flexibility to manipulate data and produce reports. The data farm will be a companion to the library's homegrown ERM system, thereby leveraging work that has already been done by providing searches according to subject area, selector, and time period. For example, such reports might show the usage of all history journals or science databases, and thus indicate trends in the use of specific subject literatures. The installation of Webtrends, a Web analytics software solution, will enable librarians to better understand how the library's Web site is used by providing answers to such questions as whether users prefer to use subject Web pages or online tutorials to learn more about the electronic resources that the library provides.[4]

Despite the level of attention given to usage statistics and the work that has been done at Yale, the data received is still quite primitive. In the future, Yale would like to obtain better information on linking between electronic resources so that informed decisions could be made based on the quality of the electronic resources. It is still difficult to determine how different groups use electronic resources, how users navigate from one resource to another, and whether they are making use of such linking tools as SFX and CrossRef. In addition, Yale librarians have no feedback or reliable data to indicate whether users are accessing the best databases for their particular subjects or using resources that will give them optimum results. As librarians assist users in person and implement new services to exploit the potential of the available databases, they must pay attention to these issues. If a better grasp of success rates in database searching could be obtained, it would be possible to determine whether additional emphasis needs to be placed on instruction and training or whether some resources require less staff intervention than others. The ability to reveal usage trends across subject areas, regardless of the vendor or source of the data, would be helpful in making collection decisions. The creation of a data farm will help accomplish this goal. As more vendors provide usage statistics and codes of practice, like those adopted by Project COUNTER, are implemented, more publishers will understand and respond to the data needs of libraries. As libraries develop local digital collections, they will begin to gather statistics in order to determine the cost effectiveness and fiscal viability of the projects. The experience libraries gain in capturing and maintaining vendor- and publisher-provided statistics will stand them in good stead as they design statistical indicators for locally created electronic resources.

The importance of creating and collecting the right kind of usage data for electronic resources is clear, but the energy required to understand and compare them makes their value debatable. Efforts to encourage vendors and publishers to provide standardized statistics will doubtlessly pay off. While not as comprehensive as might be desired, Yale's current e-resource usage statistics serve as one component that the library staff uses when evaluating electronic resources. Although usage statistics cannot indicate user satisfaction, they do show that the use of electronic resources is increasing every month. In the future, better usage statistics, more flexible tools, and more thoughtful analysis will help librarians better understand both how electronic resources are used and how collection decisions should be made.

REFERENCE NOTES

1. This information is only available to authorized users of Yale University Library.
2. Association for Research Libraries, "E-Metrics: Measures for Electronic Resources," (Washington, D.C.: ARL, 2005). Accessed 16 April, 2005, www.arl.org/stats/newmeas/emetrics.
3. Project COUNTER. Accessed 16 April, 2005, www.projectcounter.org.
4. WebTrends Web site. Accessed 16 April, 2005, www.webtrends.com.

Preservation
of Digital Resources

GEORGE MACHOVEC

The preservation and perpetual availability of digital resources continues to be one of the nagging concerns in the library and scholarly community. Librarianship, by definition, deals with the collection, organization, dissemination, and preservation of materials for a particular constituency. In the print world, libraries have well-defined practices and procedures for preserving print resources even if these efforts are usually underfunded.

In a September 1, 2001 article in *Library Journal* titled "Moving from Books to Bytes," Andrew Richard Albanese documents the "dramatic shift toward digital resources" taking place in libraries.[1] Libraries are spending larger portions of their materials budget for databases, electronic journals, and e-books. As this technological shift unfolds what will be left of this legacy even a decade into the future?

Symptoms of the Problem

The U.S. government documents program is rapidly moving away from distributing printed documents to making them electronically available on the Web. J. Edward Lee stated, "documents—government and archival—pose special problems. The *Congressional Record*, federal statutes, reports of various agencies, lose nothing when they are transferred to digital format. But the raw material of history—letters, diaries, journals, full of emotion, would be mutilated if they were reconstituted in smaller, more compact cyber form."[2] Lee's statement is not fully correct. After September 11, 2001, the U.S. government removed access to a suite of publicly available documents that were deemed sensitive in nature. Although it may have seemed prudent at the time, this action sets the stage for serious problems with after-the-fact government censorship when public materials are withdrawn because of changes in the international arena, public policy, perceptions of right and wrong, and whims of government opinion.

The United States Government Printing Office (GPO) announced that by late 2007 it will have implemented its digital content system, which will collect, preserve, and disseminate virtually all government information in digital form. By 2008 the GPO hopes to have digitized approximately 70 percent of its historical content dating back to the *Federalist Papers* in 1787.[3]

In an October 29, 1999 news release, Elsevier Science announced its new policy on the permanent archiving of its electronic journals. The company promised that it would maintain journals offered through its ScienceDirect service in perpetuity. The press release goes on to say that the "archives will be migrated, as the technology for storage, display, or access changes, and an internal production archive separate from the ScienceDirect distribution platform will ensure redundancy and the ability to recreate the files in case of disaster."[4] Derk Haank, then chief executive of Elsevier Science stated "we are keenly aware of our responsibility to assure both our subscribers and our authors that the journal literature be available and accessible indefinitely."[5] Nevertheless, on March 21, 2003, Elsevier issued a press release on its article withdrawal policy in which it cites such reasons for article removal as, "infringements of professional ethical codes, multiple submission, bogus claims of authorship, plagiarism, fraudulent use of data or the like; legal limitations upon the publisher, copyright holder, or the author(s); the identification of false or inaccurate data that, if acted upon, would pose a serious health risk."[6] Another problem recently cited by librarians focuses on continued access to content should a journal be sold to another publisher. The new publisher may not continue the original archiving policies and may not honor certain rights of access that a library had received under the terms of the original access agreement (e.g., the library may have received the journal as part of a package in a consortial deal; once the journal has been sold, access may be discontinued because its use was based on the package deal and not on a direct subscription).

Accessing a specific electronic journal published in the mid-1990s by a small organization that no longer exists can be a challenge. In the mid-1990s the Committee on Institutional Cooperation started an archiving program for small at-risk titles, but the project was terminated because most of the journals could be found elsewhere on the Web.[7] A Web search reveals announcements about the journal, reprints of individual articles, and excerpts of articles, but nowhere is there a complete run of the title. This is somewhat reminiscent of the portions of classical Greek and Roman literature, for which references and excerpts are scattered throughout other works (so an original must have existed), but the actual artifact is now lost.

On February 25, 2000, United States Court of Appeals for the Second Circuit handed down its final decision in the *Tasini v. New York Times Co.* copyright case that dealt with the electronic redistribution of articles written by freelance authors.[8] In the ruling, the court overturned a lower court decision and gave freelance writers new rights with regard to republishing their articles in electronic database aggregations.[9] Specifically, the judges ruled that a publisher may not automatically grant rights to an aggregator to electronically redistribute an article without the author's permission. According to the ruling, the publisher of electronic content does not have the same protection from copyright infringement as the publisher of other types of collections. Since the ruling was handed down, aggregators and publishers have removed content from their electronic databases if they did not have explicit permission from authors to redistribute the content in electronic form.

In the print world, everything cannot, and probably should not, be saved. However, the computer industry has become so blasé that as new hardware and software are introduced, older information may be compromised or lost. Although there are instances when data has been migrated to a new environment, it is often only done only when it is easy or economically required.

According to Jeffrey Rothenberg in his report to the Council on Library and Information Resources "the scope of this problem extends beyond the traditional library domain, affecting government records, environmental and scientific baseline data, documentation of toxic waste disposal, medical records (whose lifetime must exceed one hundred years), corporate data (such as the documentation of drug trials for pharmaceutical companies or of geologic survey data for petrochemical companies), electronic commerce transactions, and electronic records needed to support forthcoming digital government initiatives."[10] It was widely recognized that virtually all of the raw data collected during the Apollo space program in the 1960s and early 1970s is no longer available, as it was archived on 9-track tape for which readers no longer exist, even if the tapes themselves were still readable.

Issues with Archiving Digital Data

One of the most obvious and immediate problems with archiving digital data has to do with technological obsolescence. This difficulty manifests itself in several ways:

Hardware becomes obsolete and is no longer supported by developers. Some of the following storage formats are no longer available or are rarely used: paper tapes, 9-track tapes, 8-inch floppy drives,

5.25-inch floppy drives, 3.5-inch drives, large-format laser discs, and Zip drives.

Files created with such software as Visicalc, Ami Pro, Lotus, Harvard Graphics, Word Star, Paradox, Dbase, and a host of other popular programs may be difficult to use. In another decade or so, this will have become even more problematic.

Hardware and software are inextricably interconnected, and it is increasingly uneconomical to provide backward compatibility to all previous formats and structures of data. Not only does one need the right version of an application to read many files but that application must be loaded on the appropriate operating system designed for the underlying hardware on which it is mounted.

Longevity of storage media has haunted the industry for many years. Magnetic-based storage systems must be regularly refreshed. The stability of CD-ROMs and DVDs is still not well-understood but is known to be limited. Paul Conway, head of the preservation department at Yale University has noted, "our capacity to record information has increased exponentially over time while the longevity of the media used to store the information has decreased equivalently."[11] Sumerian tablets and Egyptian papyri from thousands of years ago are still readable, but a 5.25-inch floppy disk from only a decade ago can no longer be deciphered!

Authentication and security systems intended to prevent unauthorized use and copying may become an obstacle to usability and preservation. Legitimate users may be locked out of digital content and librarians will be prevented from undertaking legitimate archival endeavors.

Migrating digital data will be the key to keeping information readable and viable for future generations. To migrate data, the storage media and the format of the data must be continually updated. Migrating data to modern storage media will help maintain the integrity of the data, and ensuring that the data is in a digital format that remains widely readable with current software is crucial for usability. Although the cost of digital storage media continues to drop, the real cost comes from the human effort and organizational resolve in supporting these migrations.

There are also substantial legal issues in the digital economy. Changing copyright laws and concepts of ownership continue to threaten digital media. The publishing and entertainment industries are enthralled with short-term leasing and viewing possibilities, but such concepts as pay-per-view, self-destructing

DVDs, and similar technologies have a dark side in terms of ownership and data longevity. Concerns exist on both sides of the fence, but evolving public policy and legislation must continue to keep the needs and interests of all parties in view. The mission of libraries is collecting, preserving, and maintaining content in all media formats, while publishers are largely driven by economic interests. The natural tension that exists between these two missions means that a balance must be found between them. In the copyright arena, libraries have a long and well-developed set of guidelines regarding fair use that has been tested in the courts. However, many of the paradigms that existed in the print environment are being challenged and redefined in the digital environment.

Who Should Be Responsible?

Digital information has many stakeholders, including authors, publishers, vendors and other redistributors of content, libraries, and end users. Who should be responsible for preserving and maintaining access to this information?

In the print environment, libraries have played the role of preservation agent because they are publicly funded and not profit-driven, are politically neutral, have storage facilities and staff with expertise, and are charged with a mission to collect, organize, preserve, and disseminate information. In the digital economy this role is not so clear. Libraries often do not have the fiscal resources, technical expertise, digital storage capacity, or access to the digital data that may or may not be locally stored. Much of a library's digital content is leased and not owned, taking the library out of the loop with regard to preservation.

Publishers own content they have acquired from the creators (authors), but for-profit publishers give top priority to the bottom line and anything that becomes a drain on profitability is considered expendable. In the print environment, when books and journals go out-of-print, libraries still retain their copies and continue to provide access to them. In the digital environment, libraries no longer control access to the content and instead are at the mercy of publishers and database providers for maintaining access to the content. If a publisher decides, for a host of reasons, not to migrate or properly maintain content, the information could very easily be lost forever.

A number of library consortia, academic institutions, and other organizations (e.g., OCLC) have begun to work with publishers to provide storage and access solutions for digital content. Unfortunately, these solutions are limited due to inadequate funding, the inability of the parties to forge agreements with publishers and archiving organizations, and by the publishers' limited scope. For example, the OCLC Electronic Collections Online (ECO) project provides archiving for a body of scholarly journals but largely ignores trade and industry serials. In 2001, Yale University announced a project to archive more than 1,100 Elsevier Science journals and other organizations (e.g., University of Toronto, OhioLINK, Los Alamos National Laboratories) have loaded Science Direct journals locally.[12] Replicating digital content provides an important safety net, but the future of these projects entirely depends on whether the institutional mission of the host organizations continues to support this activity and whether the organizations will continue to provide the necessary funding.

The Library at Alexandria was one of the wonders of the ancient world that collected and preserved manuscripts from around the world. It had one major failing—the collection was maintained in only one place, so that when a series of disasters destroyed the library, the collection was lost. The same danger exists in the digital age. If data are stored in only one central repository, they are in grave danger. The Lots of Copies Keep Stuff Safe (LOCKSS) project at Stanford University has often been cited as one approach to preserving the content of electronic journals.[13] By storing copies of the journals at a number of institutions, the project accomplishes the goal of preserving data in the event of a natural disaster or other calamity and at the same time provides persistent access to the content. However, the project does not address the long-term preservation considerations of the content. "If a format is obsolescent now, it will still be obsolescent in the future."[14]

There is no simple answer to the question of who is responsible for guaranteeing ongoing preservation of and access to digital information. Almost every study and analysis on the subject concludes with proposals and recommendations that involve many different stakeholders, yet one of the big concerns is that no one is stepping up to take responsibility.

As the digital landscape continues to evolve and become more complex with shifting technologies, new laws, and new economic considerations, libraries need to take a key role as watchdogs for preservation and access. Specifically, libraries should monitor various archiving projects and programs so that if key players appear to be at risk or should fail, alternative arrangements or replacements can be introduced. As primary source material in local archives is digitized and as academic libraries begin digitizing research produced by their faculty, digital institutional repositories are being created. It is critical that they are established in accordance with best practices for data storage, migration, replication, metadata description, and access.

Framework for Good Digital Collections

In November 2001 a forum of experts was convened by the Institute of Museum and Library Services (IMLS) to develop guidelines to successfully implement and manage digitization projects.[15] The report from the forum was designed to "encourage institutions to plan their digitization practices strategically in order to develop collections that will be accessible and useful for the long-term, and that can integrate with other digital collections to support a growing network of broadly accessible digital information resources."[16] The report had two objectives:

1. to provide an overview of some of the major components and activities involved in creating good digital collections; and

2. to provide a framework for identifying, organizing, and applying existing knowledge and resources to support the development of sound local practices for creating and managing good digital collections.[17]

A second edition of the report issued in 2004 recognizes the maturation of the digital environment. This revised document includes an expanded suite of recommendations for developing digital projects that centers on good collections, good objects, good metadata, and good projects. For the purposes of the report, "goodness" is defined as much more than a simple demonstration that the concept for a digital project can be brought to fruition.

> As the digital environment . . . has matured to become a critical and often primary vehicle for delivering information . . . integration and trust have emerged as critical criteria for digital collection building. Web standards and technologies now support the integration of vast amounts of disparate information and users increasingly demand "one-stop shopping" for their information needs. Concomitantly, the vast amount of information available makes it increasingly difficult for users to find trusted information—information that is reliably available for the long-term and is known to be authentic. Objects, metadata, and collections must now be viewed not only with the context of the projects that created them but as building blocks that others can reuse, repackage, and build services upon. Indicators of goodness must now emphasize factors contributing to interoperability, reusability, persistence, verification, documentation, and support for intellectual property rights.[18]

Conclusion

As a practical measure, many libraries and consortia require statements regarding archiving or perpetual access in their contracts with primary publishers. Whether publishers will honor these contracts in the future could be in jeopardy, especially if the content is sold to another party, if an organization goes out of business, or if some unforeseen loophole materializes.

There is no simple or single solution to the preservation of digital data. In fact, different solutions may be needed, depending on intellectual property issues, the format and quantity of data, the type of software required, and other related issues. Although there are many challenges and issues associated with archiving and preserving digital data, there is no turning back. The digital revolution is here. It is crucial that librarians remain aware of the fragility of the digital environment and the need to rigorously pursue those policies that will secure and preserve the nation's intellectual heritage.

REFERENCE NOTES

1. Andrew Richard Albanese, "Moving from Books to Bytes," *Library Journal* 126, no. 14 (2001): 52–55.

2. J. Edward Lee, "Bricks, Clicks, Books, and Docs: Libraries in the Digital Age," *The Charleston Advisor* 4, no. 2 (Oct. 2002). Accessed 16 April 2005.

3. Jason Miller, "GPO Outlines Digital Conversion Plans," *Washington Technology*, 14 Dec. 2004. Accessed 16 April 2005, www.washingtontechnology.com/news/1_1/daily_news/25154-1.html.

4. George S. Machovec, "Elsevier Makes Commitment to Electronic Archiving of its Electronic Journals," *Online Libraries and Microcomputers* (Dec. 1999). Accessed 16 April 2005.

5. Ibid.

6. Elsevier, "Elsevier Policy on Article Withdrawal," *The Charleston Advisor* (Mar. 21 2003). Accessed 16 April 2005, http://charlestonco.com/pressrm/viewPR.cfm?id=393.

7. Committee on Institutional Cooperation Web site. Accessed 16 April 2005, www.cic.uiuc.edu.

8. 206 F.3d 161 (2d Cir. 2000)

9. United States District Court for the Southern District of New York.

10. Jeffrey Rothenberg, *Avoiding Technological Quicksand: Finding a Viable Technical Foundation for Digital Preservation* (Washington, D.C.: Council on Library and Information Resources, 1999), 5.

11. Paul Conway, *Preservation in the Digital World* (Washington, D.C.: The Commission on Preservation and Access, 1996), 4.

12. Elsevier, "Yale Library to Plan Digital Archives with Elsevier Science" *The Charleston Advisor* (23 Feb. 2003). Accessed 16 April 2005, http://charlestonco.com/pressrm/viewPR.cfm?id=52.

13. LOCKSS Web site. Accessed 16 April 2005, http://lockss.stanford.edu/.

14. Titia Van der Werf, "Experience of the National Library of the Netherlands," *The State of Digital Preservation: An International Perspective. Conference Proceedings April 24–25, 2002* (Washington, D.C.: Council on Library and Information Resources, 2002), 63.

15. Institute of Museum and Library Services Web site. Accessed 16 April 2005, www.imls.gov/.

16. NISO Framework Advisory Group, *A Framework of Guidance for Building Good Digital Collections*, 2d ed., (Bethesda, Md.: National Information Standards Organization Press, 2004), iv. Accessed 16 April 2005, www.niso.org/framework/framework2.html.

17. Ibid., 1.

18. Ibid.

Who Will Keep Print in the Digital Age?

Current Thinking on Shared Repositories

PAULA D. WATSON

Book storage has become a hot topic in library circles—trendy enough to attract study grants and spawn conferences. Although librarians devote a growing percentage of collection dollars to purchasing online resources, many are becoming more mindful of their responsibilities for print and other nondigital materials. The current interest in storage is driven by the same old problems and, increasingly, by concerns related to mounting reliance on electronic resources. As in the past, libraries—especially large libraries—continue to fill up with physical objects and the slow fires still burn in the stacks. However, as institutions move to license electronic resources as aggressively as their budgets allow, they often cannot afford both the print and electronic formats and increasingly see no reason to acquire the print version.

Smaller libraries trust they can eliminate hard copy versions and be reasonably secure in the expectation that the big, rich libraries will find a way to hold on to them and make them available if they are needed.[1] Certainly some number of large libraries will continue to maintain their commitment to nondigital collections, regarding the stewardship of original print collections as part of the mission that distinguishes them from lesser institutions. The continued existence of such collections is clearly a valuable insurance policy, because no one really knows yet how to create enduring archives of digital materials or what they will cost.

Although we rejoice in the benefits of electronic access, we are still drawn in a fundamentally human way to the notion of keeping accumulated knowledge safe in print, on paper, in high-density, climate-controlled buildings. Doing so offers an appealing and powerful sense of security. Librarians have traditionally thought of storage facilities as warehouses to hold low-use materials—typically back runs of journals. A shared repository may either be defined as a "unique [best] copy" depository or a place where participating libraries may send whatever they wish, even if this means that duplicates take up space on the shelves. With digital-age concerns about the mutability and impermanence of electronic objects and the vulnerability of the networks over which they are delivered, scholars and library leaders worry about creating a safety net for electronic collections. Such fail safe libraries may need to include both access archives (e.g., print runs of journals from which scans or printouts can be made as needed) and dark archives, collections that are to be used only in case of dire emergency. Both access archives and dark archives will need to be complete and in good condition if they are to serve their function in an ideal way. The evanescence of the bits and bytes that make up digital materials and the mysteries of how they will be maintained perpetually in their present, meaningful patterns have fostered a sense of urgency about creating trusted print archives of what libraries now have on their shelves or are licensing in electronic form.

Planning for a National Safety Net of Shared Print Repositories

JSTOR: Promise and Reality

Interest in developing a coordinated approach to the preservation of the original formats of library materials has been gathering force since the late 1990s, stimulated to a significant extent by the success of the Scholarly Journal Archive Project (JSTOR).[2] From the start, a key premise of JSTOR was that it would be cheaper to buy an electronic archive of major journals than to continue to maintain the print volumes of those journals on the shelf. Early marketing of JSTOR suggested that subscribers would be able to withdraw print volumes covered by the database or send them to remote locations, thus freeing shelf space.

However, libraries have not, by and large, subscribed to JSTOR titles to save storage costs. As Kevin Guthrie, board chair of JSTOR, observed in an article on the future of the project, "the primary reason for JSTOR participation seems to be not the potential savings associated with central [electronic] archiving but the benefits associated with providing better and more convenient access to the literature for faculty and students."[3] This is not especially surprising. Although JSTOR subscribers might feel reasonably comfortable relegating volumes to storage, they would find it much harder to withdraw long runs of important hardbound journals, particularly because no one at present can guarantee with complete assurance the long-term survival of JSTOR or any other electronic archive. Guthrie acknowledges that solutions to the electronic archiving problem will be costly and beyond the means of individual institutions. While he promises that JSTOR will continue to test the proposition that a not-for-profit organization can support a large-scale electronic archiving mission, Guthrie has emphasized the need to explore a variety of models for recovering the long-term costs of digital archiving.

JSTOR's sponsor, the Mellon Foundation, has taken a leadership role in exploring the technical, legal, organizational, and financial aspects of electronic archiving. In 2001 Mellon funded seven one-year electronic journal archiving projects. These studies emphasized the array of challenges involved in preserving digital resources. The findings and recommendations of the project reports have led the foundation to concentrate continuing support on two qualitatively different approaches to digital preservation: the Lots of Copies Keep Stuff Safe (LOCKSS) Project at Stanford and the new JSTOR E-Archive Initiative.[4] This new program—built on a partnership between publishers and librarians and mindful of the related work of others—aims to begin building the infrastructure needed for electronic archiving.

While pushing ahead with analyses of digital preservation issues, Mellon is also supporting the study of best practices for print archiving. JSTOR itself has become the focus of the first systematic national effort to create a distributed network of print archives as the ultimate safety net for an electronic resource. The Center for Research Libraries (CRL) is coordinating this project.

Starting the Conversation

Backstopping the JSTOR electronic collection with print is a natural extension of the historic mission of the CRL.[5] The center began collecting volumes in 2000 "to provide to the CRL members, and to the library community, assurance that paper copy of all JSTOR titles will be available as an archive."[6] In January 2001 the CRL board created the Collection Assessment Task Force to explore overall strategies for the future. The task force recommended that the center "begin now to provide leadership for the creation of a national program for the coordination of the future archiving of traditional materials." The task force proposed that CRL coordinate collection and preservation of traditional (and digital) materials among its members, as a trusted third party, by helping them to collaborate with one another.[7]

While CRL's task force worked on its report, the Council on Library and Information Resources (CLIR) sponsored a major, national-level analysis of the original format preservation question. The results of the CLIR project were published in 2001 as *The Evidence in Hand: Report of the Task Force on the Artifact in Library Collections*. This report recommended, among other things, the creation of a national network of regional repositories for "low-use print matter."[8]

Two additional grant-funded projects emphasized the potential for CRL's central role in a coordinated, national, print-preservation effort. Mellon provided support for a two-year project at CRL "to test a framework for the distributed, long-term retention of artifactual collections, using JSTOR journals as a test bed of materials." CRL is building a dark archive of JSTOR titles on-site and is coordinating the creation of distributed access archives at cooperating institutions. The grant charges CRL to study the logistics of a distributed system, including the agreements and shared assumptions required to support it.[9] The second grant to CRL, from CLIR, funded a study of existing print repositories as the next step in implementing the recommendations of CLIR's report, *The Evidence in Hand.* An important goal of this effort was to explore the extent to which existing repositories "represent an emerging architecture" for a national network. The CRL study, *Developing Print Repositories: Models for Shared Preservation and Access,* was published in June 2003 and was followed in July by a conference: "Preserving America's Print Resources."[10] The speakers included representatives of repositories both in the U.S. and abroad as well as leaders of innovative projects. A full day of presentations preceded an invitation-only post-conference summit to develop plans for the future.

The discussions and action agenda developed at this meeting are available on the CRL Web site.[11] Conferees identified overarching goals, desirable characteristics for a network of shared repositories, and categories of materials most at-risk. Participants also spelled out a number of critical needs and volunteers stepped forward to begin work in two areas. As a first step in managing redundancy and identifying gaps, representatives of the University of California and the Washington Research Libraries Center will study overlap among four existing regional repositories—their own, the Research Collections and Preservation Consortium (ReCAP), and the Five Colleges Depository in Massachusetts. The CLIR will work with others to begin to develop a high-level risk management framework to help specify, for example, the number of light versus dark archives and the amount of redundancy needed for different kinds of materials. CRL will continue to take a leadership role in bringing about collaboration and disseminating information.

Regional Repositories: Issues and Obstacles

The cavalcade of conferences, reports, and grant-funded demonstrations has emphasized critical requirements for distributed print retention centers—constraints that have not been part of planning for traditional storage facilities. Safety net collections must be secure, complete, and in as near-to-perfect condition as possible. They must also be affordable and cost-effective, both as entities in themselves and as extensions of their client institutions. Among other things, in this context affordability requires eliminating duplicates and joint ownership and management of the collection.

Storage versus Archiving

In the past, storage facilities have been filled with least-used, most-easily processed materials, most often back runs of journals. Condition and completeness have not normally been matters of concern. A safety net regional print retention center, on the other hand, must assemble complete runs of serials and collections of other formats (monographs, microforms, audio and video materials) that are of archival quality.

ReCAP, a collaboration of Columbia University, New York Public Library, and Princeton University, formed to create a massive off-site shelving facility and examined what it would take to assemble a trusted archive of JSTOR journals. With the support of a Mellon grant, the group investigated the feasibility of using this facility as a regional print retention center. An important part of the project was estimating the cost of assembling both an access collection and a dark archive of 275 core JSTOR titles. Project managers first determined whether two complete runs could be put together from the holdings of these three major research libraries. The condition of a sample of existing volumes was then examined to see how well they would serve as artifactual safety net copies. The sampling process revealed various problems related to the state of the volumes:

> including detached pages, missing text, missing illustrations, missing maps, pages replaced by photocopies, issues replaced by reprints, and missing covers. Volumes dating from the mid- to late 19th century up to 1950 were generally found to be in embrittled condition. Volumes also reflected the common practice in library binding of oversewing, a process that heightens the risk of detached pages in brittle volumes. There was also evidence in some cases of extensive handling and marking.[12]

The investigators estimated that it would cost $532,000 to assemble the dark and access archives of the 275 titles. The breakdown of these costs is $200,000 to fill gaps and $332,000 in staff costs during an eighteen-month period to do the physical inspection of the volumes and to assemble them as an archive at the ReCAP facility. The condition of the pieces suggests the importance of establishing clear guidelines at the outset as to what constitutes an artifactual collection for journals of this type (e.g., is it sufficient to have photocopies of missing pages or should all pages be originals?). The ReCAP estimate does not include the potentially high cost of de-acidifying brittle copies.

Ownership

To be most cost-effective, shared repositories should be de-duplicated, best copy collections jointly owned by the library clients they serve. The participating libraries themselves should be ready to de-accession duplicates that cannot be sent to the repository in order to maximize their own on-site space savings. But withdrawals will be a problem for public institutions that are legally bound to maintain items purchased with government funds. For example, the collection stored by the University of Massachusetts (in the Five College Depository it shares with Amherst, Hampshire, Mount Holyoke, and Smith) is housed separately and duplicates to some extent the jointly-owned holdings maintained by the four private, liberal arts colleges. In a constructive approach to this limitation, the group is exploring the idea that volumes held by the university might serve as the repository copy, thus allowing withdrawal of duplicate copies in the campus libraries of the four colleges.

Though ReCAP examined the idea of becoming a regional repository for JSTOR titles, the facility does not now function as a shared repository for its three founding libraries, as each houses its own remote collection in a separate part of the facility. This arrangement points up the reluctance of major research libraries to participate in shared ownership of de-duplicated collections. The Statistics and Measurement Committee (SMC) of the Association of Research Libraries (ARL) took action to address this problem after the CRL articulated the goal of coordinating development of a network of distributed print repositories. The SMC asked its Subcommittee on Statistics to investigate "whether the ARL statistics create negative incentives for participation in national or regional book repositories" and to discuss "how ARL might best neutralize the disincentives and encourage good management practices regarding these shared collections."[13] In 2002, with the goal of encouraging better management of collections, the subcommittee began work on defining ways to count and report volumes in ARL's *Annual Statistical Survey* that are held in shared repositories serving as extensions of individual library collections. Definitions to encompass at least three categories have been under consideration. These include volumes transferred to repositories as preservation copies as well as duplicates that can be withdrawn from individual collections because the depository will maintain a preservation copy. A third category arises from electronic journal publishers' increased willingness to offer electronic access to the libraries in a consortium, so long as a single print copy of all journals is maintained by and for the group. Individual libraries want to continue to count future volumes of journals they once had in print as though they were still physically adding them to their collections. The committee has found it hard to depart from the principle of ownership and local physical access as a measure of collection size. For now, they have opted for the compromise solution of including a "volumes held collectively" reporting line in the ARL Supplementary Statistics for 2003–04. Care is taken to require the storing library to have made an investment in the items in order to count them as part of its collection:

> The defining criterion is that the library has devoted financial resources for the purchase of these items and is taking responsibility for their availability through participation in a cooperative that supports shared ownership. The library demonstrates commitment to the shared-storage facility by supporting the consortium financially through a legally binding arrangement. Include here volumes originally held and now withdrawn from the local collection because they are held in a "shared" remote storage facility starting with volumes that have been transferred during fiscal year 2003–04. Exclude volumes held collectively because they are held by other organizations such as CRL that are supported by membership dues and determination on whether to maintain membership may vary from year to year.[14]

Participating in a shared repository may also impact other measures for assessing library performance, such as circulation and interlibrary loan rates. Volume counts were also an issue in the Five College Depository in part because the consortium included the University of Massachusetts, an ARL member. College libraries were concerned about counts as well, and were reassured by the Association of College and Research Libraries (ACRL) that they would be able to go on including commonly owned volumes in the volumes-held statistics for the individual institutions.

Overall Costs

A detailed discussion of the cost and administration of state-of-the-art, high-density safety net facilities for digital libraries is beyond the scope of this article and is well-covered elsewhere.[15] A brief review highlighting some of the major expenses of collaborative storage will demonstrate, however, that the security gained from a network of electronic fail-safes will not come cheap. The projected half-million-dollar cost of assembling access and dark archives for just 275 JSTOR titles has already been mentioned. Libraries subscribe to many thousands of electronic journals and the number of volumes needing print backup will continue to increase as publishers in various disciplines digitize their back files.

While a state-of-the-art, large-capacity, off-site storage facility costs less than adding conventional library space on scarce campus real estate, planning and building one is nevertheless an expensive proposition. The ORBIS/Cascade Alliance has recently received two grants totaling $70,000—one through the federal Library Services and Technology Act program and one from the Mellon Foundation—to develop plans for a shared repository. This twenty-seven-member consortium serving libraries in Oregon, Washington, and Idaho envisions a building that will hold two million volumes at a cost of $7.6 million. Rice University will soon be completing a $7.8 million program for a structure that will hold 1.75 million book equivalents, possibly including archival boxes, videos, and maps.

The University of Illinois has just completed a $6.8 million storage facility, the first module of which will hold approximately 1.8 million volumes. Expenditures for the inventory system software, equipment, and shelving will add another $1 million or so to the total. Additional outlays will be required for binding, supplies, cataloging, processing, and cleaning items before they are stored. Four modules are planned, bringing total capacity to around 8 million volumes. Plans for requesting funds for the second module are underway—the construction cost is very roughly estimated at $4.5 million.

Cornell University Libraries (with the support of a $120,000 grant from the Mellon Foundation) has been exploring new services that might be launched in conjunction with the building of a second module of its off-site storage annex. The project, Models for Academic Support: Restructuring Organizations for Cost-effective Information Services (MAS 2010) is looking first at whether the expanded annex might serve as a regional repository for smaller colleges as well as overcrowded state university libraries. MAS 2010 is also investigating whether Cornell could function as a service bureau for a variety of libraries and entities like university presses and museums. (Services under consideration are collection development consulting, conservation, digitizing, and electronic publishing.)[16]

The ORBIS/Cascade facility was conceived to solve space shortages in Oregon academic libraries, but with the merger of the ORBIS and Cascade consortia its mission has been expanded to include the surrounding region. If Cornell's expanded annex and other new storage facilities on individual campuses become shared repositories, administrators will surely find they need to accelerate their initial timetable of phased expansions. That the Harvard Depository, which pioneered offering space at a fee to other libraries to help defray costs, no longer accepts new clients is noteworthy in this context—managers are preserving remaining space in the facility for growth of Harvard's collection. Taking on the additional responsibilities of both a dark archive and an access archive will greatly increase the amount of space needed by shared repositories in the long term. It seems unlikely that many existing high-density facilities could be easily converted to regional repositories.

The expense of operating a collaborative repository is directly related to the number of contributors and to the size and use of the collection. Proposed service models for repositories call for articles in serials to be scanned and either printed and mailed or posted online if they are not already available online. Ideally, catalog records for stored monographs will include at least tables of contents, so that chapters in books can be treated in the same way as articles in journals. These are labor-intensive activities. Currently, depositories functioning on a fee-based business model charge client libraries according to formulas that factor in use of the stored collection. For example, the New England Regional Depository Library levies a surcharge if a library retrieves more than 4 percent of its collection in a given year.[17]

Shared repositories will also have high administrative costs, because they will need governance structures, and probably selection and policy committees. A national network of shared repositories will require yet another level of bureaucracy including mechanisms for monitoring and auditing to assure compliance with standards. The freely given mutual support that has been traditional for the most part in cooperative library ventures will, of necessity, give way to a more carefully regulated environment not unlike the licensing regime that governs electronic resource acquisition.

The language of the agreements that Yale and Michigan State have made with CRL to serve as distributed regional depositories for titles in the JSTOR collection illustrates this point. Though Yale's memorandum of agreement with the center is a simple one-page document, it contains the kind of language that typically appears in licenses with a commercial vendor for access to an electronic resource. Yale agrees, for example, "to make reasonable efforts" to obtain issues that may become missing or damaged in *Philosophical Transactions of the Royal Society*, the suite of titles it has agreed to archive. The library has signed on to shoulder the archiving responsibility for five years. Yale must notify CRL no later than six months before the agreement is due to expire should it not wish to renew.[18]

The Michigan State contract is far more elaborate, consisting of nine pages that specify obligations within the framework of a consortium. The form calls for a twenty-five-year commitment, renewable for another twenty-five years. The document, developed as a model, specifies that every reasonable measure be taken to protect the material. The library serving as a repository must agree to house the archive in a secure facility, preferably a closed stack, and to tag items with antitheft devices. Items must be checked for completeness after each use. To assure that obligations are met, the agreement specifies that depositories will be certified at regular intervals after the agreement becomes effective: first, from twelve to fourteen months and then after three years, five years, and ten years. Depositories may also be audited at any time.[19] The Michigan State document demonstrates the kind of strict guarantees that libraries may demand before they are willing to trust others to supply what is no longer on their own shelves. It also illustrates the costs involved in archiving, both for the institution responsible and for whatever agency takes on the job of certifying depositories.

Promising Models

University of California System

Perhaps the most advanced concept of how a large-scale regional depository might work has been developed by the University of California system, which has a long and effective tradition of centralized strategic planning.[20] In the early '80s the California system broke new ground for two large-scale storage facilities to serve libraries in the northern and southern parts of the state. These facilities have fairly rapidly evolved toward the concept of a University of California collection built and managed by and for all member libraries. Serious consideration of the archive function began in 2000. A major challenge, especially in the current state economic climate, will be transforming the existing repositories from storage sites holding a high percentage of duplicates to centrally planned and managed receptacles for shared collections.

State-centered efforts like California's seem to have the greatest potential to succeed as shared best-copy repositories. State funding, while not entirely reliable, has the advantage of coming from a central source that can designate an overarching common good. A state-managed system can define protocols to benefit all participants equally and can deal with property issues involved in de-duplicating collections. In addition, a collection that pools the library resources of a large state is likely to be able to meet most needs.

The Five College Depository

The Five College Depository project has been widely publicized as a model implementation of a shared repository on a small scale. The Five College Depository have a long history of productive cooperation that includes founding Hampshire College as a test-bed for higher-educational experimentation and designation of the Hampshire College Inter-Library Center as the location of research materials deemed impractical for a single institution to acquire and maintain.[21] When the Amherst Library was filled to bursting, plans were developed for a $29 million addition. Fortuitously, an ideal storage building (a decommissioned Strategic Air Command bunker) came on the market and the college was able to purchase it at the bargain-basement price of $510,000. When the other schools in the consortium found that they, too, were out of space, and after studying alternatives with a planning grant from Mellon, they decided to use the bunker as a shared repository and agreed (with the exception of the University of Massachusetts) to share a best-copy, jointly owned collection. The concept of joint ownership attracted grants from the Mellon Foundation, the Davis Education Foundation, and the Arthur Vining Davis Foundation to support the (most labor-intensive) first four years of operation. The result—not least because of the availability of the bunker—has been a highly economical enterprise.[22]

The Future

Almost paradoxically, libraries' increased reliance on electronic resources has focused new attention on print materials and their preservation. The inherent fragility of the digital medium has emphasized the staying power of the carefully protected print object. Economics and encouragement from publishers are also driving libraries of all sizes to abandon print journal subscriptions. Yet, despite the high percentage of budget dollars invested in online access, librarians recognize that collections will never be completely digital. Most of the world's publishing output is still in print form and collections contain older materials that are important for research, have artifactual value, and may never be digitized. Campus library buildings at institutions of all sizes continue to fill up, yet no library can buy all it needs.

These factors, dramatized by a series of grant-funded studies, have converged to awaken interest in creating a system of coordinated shared repositories. Shared collections may be defined along a continuum from those that warehouse whatever is discarded by participants to unique-copy depositories to artifactual collections of record. Research libraries are coming to think in terms of a nationally coordinated system with a relatively small number of repositories that will serve as collections of record. Foreseeable and significant costs for creating this kind of safety net will include bricks and mortar, assembling artifactual collections, changing and creating records, and providing access as needed. The organizational, political, and procedural issues will present unprecedented challenges.

The concept of the shared storage site as the research library of the future shadows the idea of high-level repositories. At an international conference of national repository libraries in 1999, Don Simpson, president of the CRL, spoke on the contribution of repositories to collection development and management. Pointing to the decline of ownership, he observed that "research libraries are exchanging some of the traditional archival imperatives for the user demands of 'information here and now.'" He viewed this tendency as an opportunity for repositories to build great, shared collections of both print and electronic materials, doing what research libraries can no longer afford to do on their own.[23] Echoing this view, the prospectus for the ORBIS/Cascade Regional Library Services Center points out that "a shared library shelving facility would quickly comprise one of the largest research collections in the Northwest."[24]

The CRL Collection Assessment Task Force report includes some significant assumptions for the future of research libraries, suggesting trends that will radically influence what libraries will retain in their own collections. The report asserts, for example, that "it is now a matter of accepted fact that most scholars do not stand a chance of reading anything approaching the totality of the materials currently published in their particular areas. . . few scholars have the time to read deeply or historically in their disciplines." The authors argue that this phenomenon will encourage librarians to become "more accepting of the fact that they cannot collect and archive nearly as much as they should." Moreover, they predict that the cost-per-use of print materials will increase to such an extent that very few libraries will be able to maintain large paper collections and that "the next generation of scholars will be far less averse to the withdrawal of paper materials than the present one."[25] Although Willis Bridegam, director of the Amherst College Library suggests that "unwanted [duplicate] copies" from the Five College Depository will be given to needy libraries around the world, it seems far more probable, given the cost of advertising the availability of gift volumes and the expense of shipping books, that withdrawals from most libraries contributing to shared repositories will be pulped.[26]

Largely for economic reasons, academic libraries—even the largest—are foregoing print copies of journals they get online, even if they have subscribed to these titles for decades. Mission statements have discarded the concept of the collection-centered library and embraced the idea of a user-centered (or perhaps more correctly, *use*-based) service. Even at leading research universities, the on-campus library may become virtual in more ways than one, morphing into an access management agent that directs users to online materials on faraway servers and imports print (or print surrogates) from distant repositories. Ghost volumes may eventually be counted as though they were really on the shelves and available for immediate and unmediated consultation. Many research libraries that were comfortable building just-in-case collections twenty years ago have grown increasingly accustomed to the just-in-time model advocated through the 1990s. In fact, all but an elite handful may be moving inexorably toward what might be called a just-for-now mission in the twenty-first century.

REFERENCE NOTES

1. Amy K. Weiss, John P. Abbott, and Joseph C. Harmon, "Print Journals: Off Site? Out of Site? Out of Mind?" *The Serials Librarian* 44 (2003): 274. One far-sighted

collections librarian at a smaller institution, John P. Abbott at Appalachian State University, is definitely planning to weed his collection down to what is actually used and to rely on larger libraries to supply whatever may be needed later. Recognizing that the big libraries will need help meeting the cost of maintaining huge storage facilities, he has also suggested that "small and medium-sized libraries [could] contribute a small amount (perhaps $0.10) per volume for each volume withdrawn from the smaller library's collections. These funds would be collected by the cataloging utility as part of the symbol removal and the funds transferred, as either endowment or liquid assets, to the large in-state or regional academic library that agrees to aggressively store and make available low-use books and journals."

2. Roger C. Schonfeld, *"JSTOR: A History"* Web site (Princeton, N.J.: Princeton Univ., 2003). Accessed 17 April 2005, www.jstor.org. Originally conceived by William G. Bowen, President of The Andrew W. Mellon Foundation, JSTOR began as an effort to reduce the strain on libraries caused by the need to provide adequate stack space for back runs of scholarly journals. The basic idea was to convert the older volumes of paper journals into electronic formats, producing savings in space (and the capital costs associated with that space) while simultaneously improving access to journal content. Libraries would also be relieved of expenses related to the preservation of paper volumes. Referenced volume contains the full story of JSTOR, a list of articles on the project, and other details.

3. Kevin M. Guthrie, "Archiving in the Digital Age: There's a Will, But Is There a Way?" *EDUCAUSE Review* 36 (Nov./Dec. 2001): 56–65. Accessed 17 April 2005, www .educause.edu/LibraryDetailPage/666?ID=ERM0164.

4. LOCKSS Web site. Accessed 17 April 2005, http://lockss.stanford.edu; JSTOR, "JSTOR Archiving Practices."Accessed 17 April 2005, www.jstor.org/about/archive.html.

5. Center for Research Libraries, "Historical Background to 1980" (Chicago: CRL, 2005). Accessed 17 April 2005, www.crl.edu/content.asp?l1=1&l2=29. The Center for Research Libraries was founded in 1949 as the Midwest Inter-Library Center (MILC), a cooperative storage and distribution center for little-used books from the collections of thirteen university libraries in the region. Reconceived as the Center for Research Libraries in 1965, it took on a national role, a greatly expanded membership, and new functions including cooperative purchase and preservation programs.

6. Center for Research Libraries, "CRL's JSTOR Archives" (Chicago: CRL, 2005). Accessed 17 April 2005, www.crl.edu/content.asp?l1=4&l2=19&l3=35&l4=62&l5= 12#goals.

7. Center for Research Libraries, "Historical Background to 1980."

8. *The Evidence in Hand: Report of the Task Force on the Artifact in Library Collections* (Washington, D.C.: Council on Library and Information Resources, 2001). Accessed 17 April 2005, www.clir.org/pubs/reports/pub103/pub103.pdf.

9. Ross Atkinson, "Report of the Collection Assessment Task Force" (Chicago: Center for Research Libraries, 2001). Accessed 17 April 2005, www.crl.edu/content.asp?l1=1&l2= 9&l3=13&l4=1.

10. Bernard F. Reilly, *Developing Print Repositories: Models for Shared Preservation and Access* (Washington, D.C.: Council on Library and Information Resources, 2003).

11. CRL, "Preserving America's Print Resources: Toward a National Strategic Effort Report on the Planning Day Discussions," in *Library Collections, Acquisitions, and Technical*

Services 28 (spring 2004): 5–78. Accessed 17 April 2005, www.crl.edu/content/ PAPRreportdraft.pdf. Future needs, problems, roles of different stakeholders are explored in some depth in the background and action agenda.

12. James G. Neal, "The ReCAP Artifactual Repository Planning Project," *Library Collections, Acquisitions, and Technical Services* 28 (spring 2004): 25–28.

13. ARL, "Proposed Changes to the ARL Data Collection Activities" (Washington, D.C.: ARL 2003). Accessed 17 April 2005, www.arl.org/stats/program/2003/a3_proposal.pdf.

14. The quoted paragraph is from the *ARL Supplementary Statistics 2003–04 Survey* at www.arl.org/stats/mailing/m04/04ssurvey.pdf. Information on efforts to address statistics issues related to ownership of volumes in shared repositories may be found on the ARL Web site in the minutes of the ARL Statistics and Measurement Committee meeting included as part of membership meetings on October 16, 2002 in Washington, D.C. (www.arl.org/stats/program/2003/min1002.pdf) on May 14, 2003 in Lexington, Kentucky (www.arl.org/stats/program/2003/0503min.pdf) and on May 12, 2004 in Tucson (Arizona www.arl.org/stats/program/2004/ min0504.pdf). See also the ARL Statistics and Measurement Committee *Activities Report 2003*. Accessed 17 April 2005, www.arl.org.stats/program/2003/agnd1003.htm.

15. Useful recent contributions to the literature include: Danuta A. Nitecki and Curtis L. Kendrick, eds., *Library Off-site Shelving: Guide for High-density Facilities* (Englewood, Colo.: Libraries Unlimited, 2001). A comprehensive manual for storage building planners. *Developing Print Repositories* describes existing repositories that serve as more than single-institution storehouses both inside and outside the U.S., and includes a detailed discussion of issues related to collaborative storage.

    David Weeks and Ron Chepesiuk, "The Harvard Model and the Rise of Shared Storage Facilities," *Resource Sharing & Information Networks* 16 (2002): 159–68. Describes the high-density storage facilities belonging to three consortia.

    Steve O'Connor et al. "A Study of Collaborative Storage of Library Resources" *Library Hi-Tech* 20 (2002): 258–69. A review of the collaborative storage situation in the United Kingdom, a description of facilities in various countries, an overview of major issues, and an excellent bibliography.

16. Description of Cornell's MAS 2010 project. Accessed 17 April 2005, www.library .cornell.edu/MAS/.

17. Accessed 17 April 2005, www.nelinet.net/deposit/prospectus.htm.

18. Accessed 17 April 2005, www.crl.edu/JSTORTitles/PDFs/Yale_Contract.pdf.

19. Accessed 17 April 2005, www.crl.edu/JSTORTitles/PDFs/MSU_Contract.pdf.

20. Brian E. C. Schottlaender, "You Say You Want an Evolution . . . : The Emerging UC Libraries Shared Collection," *Library Collections, Acquisitions, and Technical Services* 28 (spring 2004): 13–24.

21. The Hampshire College Inter-Library Center was closed during a period when the sponsoring institutions had sufficient space to house needed materials.

22. A full description of the project can be found in Willis E. Bridegam, *A Collaborative Approach to Collection Storage: The Five-College Library Depository* (Washington, D.C.: Council on Library and Information Resources, June 2001). Accessed 17 April 2005, www.clir.org/pubs/reports/pub97/pub97.pdf.

    For a report of shared repository planning at another set of small colleges, see Judy Luther, et al., *Library Buildings and the Building of a Collaborative Research Collection at the Tri-College Library Consortium* (Washington, D.C.: Council on

Library and Information Resources, 2003). Accessed 17 April 2005, www.clir.org/pubs/reports/pub115/pub115.pdf.

23. Don Simpson, "How Repository Libraries Contribute Effectively to the Fabric of Collection Development and Management," in Pauline A. Connolly, ed., *Solving Collection Problems through Repository Strategies: Proceedings of an International Conference held in Kuopio, Finland, May 1999* (Wetherby, West Yorkshire U.K.: IFLA Offices for Universal Availability of Publications and International Lending, 1999).

24. Orbis Cascade Alliance, *Regional Library Services Center Prospectus.* Accessed 17 April 2005, http://libweb.uoregon.edu/orbis/rlsc/Prospectus.html.

25. Atkinson, "Report of the Collection Assessment Task Force."

26. Bridegam, *A Collaborative Approach to Collection Storage.*

Automated Library System Vendors and Electronic Resources Management

An Outline of Requirements

RICHARD W. BOSS

As libraries of all types subscribe to a steadily increasing number of electronic resources, managing the licenses of those resources is becoming a major headache; so much so that a number of libraries have created in-house databases to help them control their licenses. While these in-house databases have allowed libraries to gain a modicum of control over the licenses, they have also increased the amount of duplication in the data entry required for implementing and maintaining one more system.

In seeking a turnkey solution to this management problem, a number of libraries have turned to the vendor of their integrated library system (ILS) for help. Logically, ILS vendors can supply an electronic resources management (ERM) product because ERM systems share many features with the technical services modules of ILS and because much of the database information may be found in the library portal, which is a component of many ILS. Several ILS vendors are developing, or have announced the intention to develop, an ERM system, either integrated with the library system, as a stand-alone product, or both.

Requirements for ERM

Libraries planning to implement an ERM system should incorporate the following requirements into planning and designing the system.

The information in this appendix is based on a presentation made at the ALCTS Midwinter Symposium "Taming the Electronic Tiger: Effective Management of E-resources," held in San Diego in January 2004.

Database Name

The name of the database should be that which appears on the license. Variants of the name, including the name of a related print version (if any) should also be included.

Content

A description of the content should include the breadth and length of coverage of the database. If a backfile is available but not included in the license agreement, details about that content should also be specified.

Producer, Licensor, and Aggregator

In order to eliminate confusion, the producer, licensor, and aggregator of the database should be clearly identified. Specificity will help avoid confusion in instances when the producer may have entered into an arrangement with another organization for content delivery.

Packaging

Many databases, whether from the same source or from different sources, may be combined in packages. E-journals from multiple sources are frequently packaged together. Libraries need to access records by both the database name and the package the database comprises. Packages, especially packages of journal titles, often consist of a great number of resources, therefore it is important that libraries are able to itemize the contents of the package.

License Duration and Renewal Alert

The beginning and ending dates of the license must be clearly specified and a renewal alert should be generated at least ninety days prior to the expiration of the license.

Copy of Contract

In addition to a printed copy of the contract, an electronic copy of the contract should be part of the record. A keyword-searchable version of the contract is more useful than a PDF version.

Price and Payment Terms

Details about the price, including the basis for the price, should be included along with the payment schedule.

Payment History

The record should include payment dates, amounts paid, and voucher or check numbers.

Access Methods and Resource Links

All access methods should be specified and all uniform resource locators (URLs) should be itemized.

Access Restrictions

Information regarding access restrictions, such as whether remote users with library ID numbers can access the resource or whether access is limited to a specific workstation in the library, should be described.

Contact History

Details of all communications with the producer, provider, and aggregator, including the date and subject of the communication, should be recorded, as should any decisions that may have been reached.

Use Statistics and Cost per Use

Use statistics should be available to library staff, as should a means of calculating the cost per use by dividing the annual subscription price by the number of uses. While that data may not indicate the usefulness of an electronic resource, it may help to pinpoint which resources are expensive relative to their use.

Who Sees What

All the information in the ERM system must be accessible to individuals responsible for managing the contracts. Furthermore, various subsets of the information, such as journal holdings statements, access URLs, printing permissions, and interlibrary loan policies should be available to all library staff and patrons. Access to the information should be controlled by a multitiered system of authorization and security.

The Digital Library Federation's Electronic Resource Management Initiative issued *Electronic Resource Management: The Report of the DLF Initiative*, which outlines the state of ERM and specifies in detail the functional requirements for ERM.[1]

REFERENCE NOTE

1. Digital Library Federation, "DLF Electronic Resource Management Initiative" (Washington, D.C.: DLF, 2004). Accessed 17 April 2005, www.diglib.org/standards/dlf-erm02.htm.

Contributors

Pamela Bluh
Associate Director for Technical Services & Administration
Thurgood Marshall Law Library
University of Maryland
pbluh@umaryland.edu

Richard W. Boss
Senior Consultant
Information Systems Consultants Inc.
dickboss@erols.com

Tim Bucknall
Assistant Director
Walter Clinton Jackson Library
University of North Carolina at Greensboro
bucknall@uncg.edu

Cindy Hepfer
Head, Electronic Periodicals Management Dept.
Central Technical Services
University at Buffalo (SUNY)
HSLcindy@buffalo.edu

Sandy Hurd
Director of Sales, Digital Solutions
Innovative Interfaces, Inc.
shurd@iii.com

Timothy D. Jewell
Collection Management Services
University of Washington Libraries
tjewell@u.washington.edu

George Machovec
Associate Director
Colorado Alliance of Research Libraries
gmachove@coalliance.org

Norman S. Medeiros
Coordinator of Bibliographic & Digital
    Services
Magill Library
Haverford College
nmedeiro@haverford.edu

Robert Molyneux
Chief Statistician
Sirsi Corporation
drdata@molyneux.com

Dan Tonkery
Vice President of Business Development
EBSCO Information Services
dtonkery@ebsco.com

Beth Forrest Warner
Assistant Vice Provost for Information
    Services
Director, Digital Library Initiatives
University of Kansas
bwarner@ku.edu

Paula Watson
Director for Scholarly Communication
University of Illinois at Urbana-
    Champaign
pdwatson@uiuc.edu

Jennifer Weintraub
Digital Collections Specialist
Yale University Library
Jennifer.weintraub@yale.edu

Friedemann Weigel
Managing Partner & Director
Information Systems
Harrassowitz
fweigel@harrassowitz.de

Printed in the United States
45925LVS00007B/151-453

9 780838 983669